Travel Stories and Highlights

2019 Edition

Originally published on the *Fred's Diary 1981* blog

Edited by Robert Fear

Table of Contents

Introduction

A warm welcome to this third annual anthology of travel stories and highlights.

This latest book is the biggest and best yet. It contains 66 travel stories (500-1000 words) and 66 travel highlights (50-100 words) from 55 authors, writers and poets.

2018 is the fourth year in which I have run travel writing competitions on the fd81.net blog. The stories and highlights in this book have been selected from entries to those contests.

They take you to all corners of the globe and showcase the talents of well-known travel memoirists, experienced travel writers and rising stars in the travel writing world.

I hope that you enjoy this fantastic new collection.

Robert Fear

December 2018

TRAVEL STORIES

A Koh Samui Shirt
by Mark Boyter

My Koh Samui shirt died. My John K shirt. Pulled it over my head instead of unbuttoning it and ripped it shoulder to shoulder. It was old and blotched and faded and threadbare, and I guess it's time had just come, although in fairness it wasn't particularly thread-thick to begin with.

Made from a rice sack. Dyed purple with three large red Thai letters I always assumed was the company name but could have said rice. In the sun, the purple faded into the colour of the cream after a bowl of summer blueberries, and the red letters that had given the shirt its soul clouded over in the milkiness and then were gone.

I met John K in China in Leshan. Summer of '88. We were there to see the giant stone Buddha. John K was a beautiful young high school History teacher, with long wavy blond hair and piercing blue eyes from Frederick, Maryland. I was a month out of teaching in Japan. Nagoya. He had been in Asia the previous summer. Thailand. Hong Kong. Vietnam. This summer, Hong Kong again and now China. I'd been in Asia 28 months and was on my long, hard way home. The shinkansen south to Kagoshima, the boat to Okinawa milk-running its way through the islands in the East China Sea, then the boat to Kaohsiung, Taiwan. Then Hong Kong and up the Pearl River into China and make my way to Beijing and then overland west to Urumqi and Pakistan and finally Europe. That was the plan at least. What did I know? I was young.

China in July was stiflingly hot with overwhelming humidity, and while Chinese travel could be many things, what it always was, was arduous, and by the time our train made Beijing, neither of us had the energy or desire to embrace ardu anymore.

"There's this place," he said over dinner, and his eyes brightened. "I was there last year. Long golden beaches. Palm trees. Cocoanut and papaya milk shakes. And long skewers of barbequed shrimp," and he held out his hands and I believed him. "Koh Samui," he said. "In the Gulf of Thailand. Nature Bungalows. Mae Nam beach. 50 baht a night for a hut, right on the beach. You open your door and there you are. A dollar-fifty. And girls. Beautiful girls. And long skewers of barbequed shrimp," and he held out his arms again, and I believed even more. "The night bus from Bangkok to Surat Thani, then the boat and you're there. It's easy." And he looked at me. "Long skewers of shrimp."

When he said he wasn't going to spend his last three weeks of vacation here, that he was taking the train to Hong Kong and buying a ticket to Thailand, I said yes. And he was right. About everything.

One day we rented 80cc bikes. 150 baht a day. $5. There was a shirt shop, he said, on the south-east side of the island, near Lamai Beach. A couple of Thai grandmothers ran it. Sewing machines in the back of the shop, piles of rice sacks beside. He'd bought two last year. He wanted more, for himself and for gifts. I loved the ride. I passed on the shirts.

When John K left Samui, I left too; a ten-day Vipassana retreat at Wat Suan Mokkh, 40 minutes north of Surat Thani. On the eleventh morning I bowed good-bye and walked to the highway and flagged down a local bus and bought a boat ticket and caught the Mae Nam songthaew and pushed the buzzer at Nature Bungalows and got a hut on the beach and strung up a clothes line and stayed for 17 new days, looking into the turquoise water. It wasn't the same without John K, but it wasn't supposed to be. A pliancy set in, an acceptance. A new circadian rhythm that came with the sunrise and the delicate kumquat air of first tropical light before settling into mid-day sun and heat and a fiery demanding sunset and the enveloping blackness of night and then sleep and then again. In those new easy solitary days, I rented an 80cc bike and rode back to that shop and bought two shirts, one mauve, one green.

I saw John K once more, in Kathmandu the next October. He'd told me he was taking a sabbatical and Nepal was on his list. I'd gone to Nepal the October after Samui and trekked Annapurna. The shirts were perfect; they weighed little in my pack, and I could layer both if I needed warmth. One hot morning I stopped to rest at a river and stripping off in the sun I laid the green one, soaked with sweat, on a boulder to dry and it blew off in an eddy of wind into the water and was gone.

I returned to Nepal in '89 to do Everest and Langtang and I wondered, looking every day on the off-chance I had learned to trust. One morning I turned a corner in Thamel and I recognised that long blond hair, and it was finding a brother and the universe saying yes to us both.

That was the last.

I got back to Canada after Samui in winter, and when spring arrived, and I put the shirt on it didn't feel right. There was no golden beach, no turquoise water and most distressingly, a different me. Whenever I cleaned my closet, I always threw it on the discard pile and then picked it up and hung it back in the closet until the next time.

When the shirt ripped, I ripped it again and then again, so I wouldn't be tempted to save it. And then I stopped and folded it and set it on the back of a chair. It's been a week now.

29 years.

It's just a cheap shirt from Koh Samui made from a rice sack that I never wore anymore.

That's what I tell myself, anyway.

Consequences
by Lindsay de Feliz

Having breakfast on a lazy Sunday morning as the sun flickered across the oak table, I looked up from the travel section of the Sunday Times.

"I want to go back to the Maldives next month," I announced to my husband.

There was a pause.

Did you hear me?"

"Yes, and I am not going with you. I am too busy and it's a waste of money," he answered gruffly. *If he hadn't said that?*

"Fine, I'll go on my own," I replied.

Three weeks later I boarded an Emirates flight to Male, Maldives via Dubai and sitting there in Business Class, sipping my champagne, the excitement bubbled up in me, mirroring the golden bubbles in the glass.

I was off to my favourite place in the world, the amazing islands of the Maldives to go scuba diving, which I adored with a passion. And I was going alone; the only person to please was myself.

My husband of ten years was a diver and we used to go to the Grenadines in the Caribbean on a live-aboard dive boat, called *Explorer.* It was a bit of an old tub of a boat, having previously been an Arctic exploration vessel, but somehow the peeling paint and odd layout added to its charm. Everything was basic but functional, from the small double cabins, to the food, to the steep, metal staircases between all the decks and there was something cosy and welcoming about the ship. I spent my time reading, lying on the beach and had no desire at all to go diving. It seemed far too dangerous to me. *If I had carried on thinking that way?*

Explorer left the Caribbean and sailed to the Maldives with the new name of *Atoll Explorer*, so we decided to go for our first visit to the Maldives.

The Maldives was simply stunning. If there is a heaven on earth, then that describes the Maldives. Twenty-six atolls made up of thousands of tiny white sandy islands surrounded by pristine clear turquoise water which turns into dark blue in the deep channels between the atolls. As far as your eyes can see the Indian Ocean is brimming with literally millions of brightly coloured fish, fabulous coral formations, eagle rays, sting rays, sharks, moray eels, turtles and manta rays. You feel like you are inside an aquarium. In another

16

world, another universe. This time I could not resist, and I learned to dive. *If I had not decided to dive?*

I didn't just like diving, I adored it. Not just the fascination with the marine life but the feeling of weightlessness. Gliding lazily through the water a feeling of pure unadulterated joy would come over me. It was like a drug and every time a dive was over, I couldn't wait to get back in the water, so over the next few years we went to the Maldives to dive twice a year.

Pressure in my ears told me the plane was descending and I eagerly looked out of the window, desperate for my first sight of the atolls scattered down below. I couldn't wait to get off the plane and was quickly through customs and immigration who smiled at me like an old friend as they looked at all of the Maldivian stamps in my passport.

"*Kihineh,*" they said in Dhivehi smiling, "How are you?"

"*Rangalhu Shukuriyaa,*" I replied. "I am fine, thank you," and strode out into the blazing sunshine, making my way along the long line of *dhonis* tied up outside the airport bobbing up and down in the water, until I reached the one for Atoll Explorer.

"Lindsay," shouting the boatman, "*Kihineh*, Welcome back"

To me it was more than a welcome back, it was a welcome home. I was home and I could feel all the stress and tension pouring out of me.

We chugged across steadily from the airport to Kurumba Island only 10 minutes away, where *Atoll Explorer* was anchored. The crew helped me aboard handing up my luggage and there were hugs and handshakes all around. I left my dive bag on the dive deck and the boys took my small squishy canvas bag of sarongs, swimsuits, cargo pants and t-shirts to my usual cabin, where bright pink petals were strewn over the bed.

Shoes off, the last time I would wear shoes for two weeks, quick change into cargo pants and a t- shirt and I was ready for my first Bloody Mary of the trip and meeting my 18 fellow passengers. The gentle swaying of the boat lulled me into a deep and dreamless sleep until dawn the next morning when the engines spluttered into life and we set off for the first dive site of the journey.

I dived two or three times a day every day. Weightless in body and mind 60 feet down in the warm ocean, it was a fabulous tapestry of a life so different from my normal busy, stressful existence, watching cleaner wrasse cleaning the teeth of a moray eel, having my fins nibbled by a friendly turtle, and floating through shoal after shoal of striped yellow snapper.

On the last night but one, we had a barbecue on a tiny little island, just a sandbank and after devouring freshly barbecued lobster I went for a walk along the edge of the water, alone. The warm water lapped my feet and the sand was like silk between my toes. Wherever I looked I could see the horizon and more stars than I ever knew existed enveloped the sky from one horizon to the other. It was simply breathtaking. A Maldivian dive instructor walked over to me and put his arm companionably around my shoulders.

"Look, Lindsay that is your constellation up there. That is Scorpio."

And it was there, at that exact moment, I made the decision to leave England, to leave my job, to leave my husband and travel the world alone as a diving instructor.

Navajo Sally and Kokopelli
by Patricia Steele

The Navajo woman's aged façade emitted grit and strength and her Indian jewelry held strands of steel gray hair tightly in a bun. I was riveted to her tawny face, which was the color of aged whiskey. Her hand gripped the vehicle's shifting post, a turquoise ring covered one finger from joint to knuckle.

Canyon de Chelly is in the Navajo Nation at the northeastern corner of Arizona. The cottonwood trees swayed above as our Navajo guide's words immersed us in her culture. Her jeep was old. After crawling up on the back bumper, I climbed over the spare tire to find a foot hold. I threw one leg over the back seat and pulled the other one behind me as I slid downward. A broken seat belt… The woman backed up and took off as I grabbed the roll bar with one hand and my camera strap with the other. She was set on go and we were ready to roll.

Golden sand gusted and settled around me. My butt gripped the back seat of the open-air Jeep as I twisted and lurched, wishing my shoulder harness had a buckle to secure it into… Wind blew through my hair as I watched the intensity of Sally's tawny-lined face in the rear-view mirror. Suddenly, after passing fenced pastures filled with horses, bridles, saddles and a few people readying for a horse tour, the magnificent panorama opened up. High reddish-ochre, granite canyon walls rose above us in a huge expanse of sand, a silt meadow.

Startled, I was curious why two other Jeeps stood side-by-side ahead of us. Did we have to wait our turn to slip ahead? Before the question sailed through my brain, Sally braked, reversed gears and stepped on the gas…back, back, back until she braked suddenly again. What? Then she threw it into drive and lurched ahead…fast! We left the other vehicles in the dust so to speak. They were stuck in the sand! A few words later, I learned she'd been stuck only twice this year; when a vehicle gets slogged down into those 8 to 10 inches of soft sand, the wheels like to cuddle down and stop. So, she raced across the deep sandy stretches and said, "Hold on." Without a working seat belt, the roll bar was my best friend.

The floor of the canyon was a surprise. A slight wind propelled dusty sand around us. Cottonwood trees were everywhere. Sally said the Russian olive trees had been removed because the canyon must remain clear for farming and tour traffic. Today, Navajo families still make their homes, raise livestock and farm the land within the canyon. Fencing was unique; small tree trunks and large branch stocks were used as posts. They were wired together to house horses, cows and to keep small animals out of their vegetable gardens.

Rolling across the ground between 20 and 30 mph felt like I was water skiing again. She avoided prior tire tracks by driving over their tufted edges to avoid sinking into the sand. Bumpy and smooth blended together, so judging when to grip the window ledge or the roll bar was tricky. Once, I actually flipped off the seat toward the open window on the other side of the Jeep. I found a foothold and wrapped the shoulder harness strap around my wrist, took a deep breath and raised my Nikon as we gazed up forever toward red and ochre rock walls. Of course I did.

Dust devils slipped around us. More sand flew. The Arizona sun stoked the canyon walls. Sally's voice softened when she talked of Navajo traditions, myths and stories while pointing out ancient pueblo sites and rock images on the sheer cliff walls. Homes were built into alcoves to take advantage of the sunlight and natural protection. With a small mirror to redirect the sun, she used it as a pointer to show us *Anasazi* petroglyphs drawn by Puebloans centuries earlier. Her words were like a chant. We saw petroglyphs of hands, people, animals and objects. I was fascinated.

My breath caught when I saw the *White House Ruin*, the most complete group of ruins. Ochre-colored buildings were snugged on a high ledge with a lone, white building. I imagined a time when Puebloans walked, worked, played and loved.

As Sally proudly described her people's past, I felt close to her mystical people and heard their music as we listened to the Navajo stories. Kokopelli was my favorite; he was the fertility deity, depicted as a humpbacked flute player. Despite being a trickster, representing the spirit of music, Kokopelli was a womanizer. Although history states that he carried seeds for agriculture and seeds of *unborn children on his back to distribute them to women,* Sally said he loved all women: He distributed seed, but they weren't from a bag on his back...

The moon eclipse? Navajos believe their people should not stare at the moon. Tradition dictates that Navajos cannot eat during an eclipse or they will have stomach problems. They should not sleep during an eclipse because their eyes won't open again. Traditional Navajos do not look at an eclipse when pregnant because their unborn child may be born deformed. Pregnant women were actually covered during moon eclipses.

When our tour ended, I white-knuckled the roll bar when Sally sailed the Jeep back over the sand. Her jaunty Kokopelli whispered through my mind as we sped along that hot, sandy trip back to the real world. At the end of the day, I hadn't flipped out of the jeep and I had a hundred photos. Despite my gritty hair riddled with sand and ripping my shorts when I slid out of the old Jeep, I still smiled. I found a silver pendant shaped like the naughty humpbacked flute player to remember Sally and *Canyon de Chelly.* And I imagine that impish character each time I slip it around my neck.

Sally

The Last Flight of Air Siam
by Syd Blackwell

Our bookings had been made for months. Our Air Siam tickets would take us from Vancouver to Honolulu, Tokyo, Hong Kong, and Bangkok. We could stop in any or all of the intermediate destinations for four days or multiples of four days. It was also the cheapest flight we could find in those long-ago, pre-computer days. It seemed ideal.

The little Chinese travel agent in the east end of Vancouver, reputedly the guy with the best deals, had been sweaty and furtive when we bought our tickets. We had mostly forgotten that detail as our travel date approached, but then we got the phone call. Our agent nervously told us Air Siam was having mechanical difficulties with the plane that flew to Hawaii and we might be delayed four days. My friend explained he was getting married in Malaysia and a delay was not acceptable. I told him to solve the problem through another carrier or we would come back to his office to hold him personally accountable. A subsequent phone call from our now-inspired agent directed us to a different airline for our scheduled date of departure.

We should have taken this omen more seriously.

Although just past my thirtieth birthday, my travelling experience had been limited to six Canadian provinces and two American states. My friend was much more travelled. He was originally from Malaysia. But, for me, Hawaii was exotic! A palm tree was exotic! The flowers were exotic! Everything was exotic! The overt commercialism of Waikiki had barely scratched my enchanted vision when we left four days later. Air Siam was available as scheduled. What could go wrong?

Our flight across the Pacific included an awesome chase of a setting sun. We landed in darkness in Tokyo. All deplaning passengers were directed to a holding room. We were asked to wait. Soon, a representative of Air Siam came to announce the airline was having "mechanical difficulties". A plane might not be available in four days. Anyone who stayed might have to be in Japan for eight days. We could stay, or we could re-board the plane for Hong Kong. Most of us returned to the plane. We never saw the others again.

Other Air Siam passengers joined the flight at Tokyo and they brought news. The rumours were that Air Siam was in serious trouble. There were no more flights scheduled from Japan to Hawaii. Some had already decided to stay on this plane right through to Bangkok. They believed it might be the last Air Siam flight. However, when we saw night-lit Kai Tak airstrip jutting out into Victoria Harbour, and saw the city lights all around, there was absolutely no question. We were staying in Hong Kong for at least four days. We would take our chances. Soon after, the last Air Siam flight ever rose through the hot humid night air towards Bangkok.

Hong Kong in the mid-1970s was not the Hong Kong of today. It was a British crown colony that felt the impending presence of giant China. A decade after my visit, I recalled that Hong Kong in this poem.

DIM SUM

The Hong Kong slideshow
on the white plaster
living room wall
was just some
Pompeii fresco
still-life tickling
of my sense
of sight
Void of the
sultry stinking
cacophonous
jostling hustling
1-cent fishball
in blackbean sauce
opiated
neon gaudy
every sailor whorehouse
camera-toting tourist
rich/poor
entrepreneurial sweatshop
Destined to die
a predetermined
1997
death

Hong Kong was in Asia, the continent of my dreams, nurtured by hundreds of National Geographics. My friend guided me into Asian ways. We had four exhilarating days, before we returned to Kai Tak in search of a flight to Bangkok.

There were dozens around the Air Siam desk. There were no flights posted. Two beleaguered employees were facing an uneasy crowd. Their message was the same as we had heard in Tokyo. There were "mechanical difficulties". We should all go away and check back tomorrow. The crowd dispersed and most left the terminal.

However, a few of us did not leave. We didn't believe tomorrow would be better. The employees knew the airline was bankrupt, but not how to deal with the problem. They were stalling.

We again approached the desk to explain my friend was travelling from Canada to Malaysia for his wedding and we could not wait. We pressed them to find us seats on some other airline. They listened and made notes and asked us to wait nearby. They handled others who had remained. While we waited, we compared our stories of urgency. In actual fact, we had no urgency. My friend's family hoped he would find a Malaysian wife and had arranged some prospects for him to meet. He had no intention of marrying one.

The day passed slowly. Most gave up and returned to the city. About eight hours later, the few remaining were called to the Air Siam desk. We were told to go to the check-in for a Pan-Am flight to Bangkok. There, we got standby boarding passes. After all other passengers were boarded, they called the standbys. We all got on; the plane was just half full. In those days, Pan-Am and TWA ran competing routes and their planes were rarely full. All the Air Siam passengers could have been transported. However, there was little likelihood that Pan-Am would ever be compensated. They possibly agreed because so few of us remained.

We did not know or care about any of this. We were just delighted to be completing the final leg of our eventful Air Siam journey, even though four days before we had been on the actual last flight of Air Siam.

POSTSCRIPT

After a week in Bangkok, we flew Malaysian Airlines to Kuala Lumpur. My friend actually married a lovely Malaysian girl in an amazing Hindu wedding. The couple returned to Canada, raised a family, and are retired in Vancouver. I continued travelling in Asia and Europe for several more months.

Terror in the Desert - Egypt 1991
by Alison Galilian

'Hurgada! Hurgada!' yelled the bus driver out the battered door. The old engine roared reluctantly to life and we were on our way at last. Perhaps I shouldn't have chosen August to travel across the desert. The sun was ferocious - the rays intensified through the glass windows, turning the non-airconditioned bus into a human oven.

A little while into the journey, the driver suddenly slammed on the brakes. We were surrounded by army trucks. A soldier hammered at the door of the bus, ordering the driver to open the doors. He came aboard holding his rifle out in front of him. His cold stare worked its way quickly and efficiently around the bus. He walked slowly up the aisle, staring at each passenger - his rifle aimed in the same direction as his eyes. No one spoke. No one dared move. The soldier turned to a passenger halfway up the aisle. He yelled angrily at him in Arabic. The terrified man began frantically searching through his pockets. I found myself willing him to find the elusive item before something far worse happened. The man eventually produced a crumpled, torn paper. The soldier snatched it from his hands then grabbed him by the collar and dragged him off the bus. I watched in horror as the man was pushed face down in the sand. Another soldier placed a foot on him, then pointed a rifle to his head. Our armed man returned. Two more passengers were dragged off the bus. I sat rigid, afraid to move in case I attracted his attention. I wished I hadn't sat in the seat facing the aisle. I wanted to cower behind a seat and be invisible. The area we were travelling through had seen its share of militia attacks and political unrest. I started to worry I might be taken hostage.

The soldier was now walking towards me. His cold eyes suddenly locked on mine. My heart was thumping so hard, it pounded in my ears. I stared back, determined not to show my fear. He walked up to me until the end of his rifle was inches from my face. He glanced quickly at the passengers on each side of me, then turned around. He shouted something at the driver before stepping off our bus. A few minutes later, the road block moved away to allow us to pass. We were on our way again. Excited chatter broke out amongst the remaining passengers, who appeared united by this terrifying ordeal.

Two hours later, thick, black smoke began belching into the bus. The engine began to splutter. The bus jolted violently forwards then ground to a halt. We were in the middle of nowhere. The driver went to inspect the engine and was soon followed by all the passengers. I took the opportunity to escape the toxic human oven and resigned myself to the fact that we had a long, hot wait. I passed the time listening to my Walkman, allowing the music to become the backdrop of my surreal movie set.

I didn't hear the jeep arrive. When I saw it skid to a stop next to the bus, I took off my headphones. A soldier got out and went to speak to the bus driver, then walked over to me. 'You! Come!', he insisted. Too afraid to argue, I grabbed my bag and was pushed into the jeep next to three other soldiers. I thought of my Dad, who was well read on Middle Eastern affairs, and who had warned me to be careful in Egypt. I imagined the phone call my parents would receive. 'Hello, we're sorry to inform you that your daughter has been taken hostage by militants whilst travelling through a volatile part of Egypt.'

The jeep moved quickly across the desert. We eventually came to a stop at a small, remote building. 'Out!', shouted the same soldier who had forced me into the Jeep. 'You stay here'. Any questions I had about what was going to happen to me were unanswered. Whether it was due to a lack of English or whether I was deliberately not being told, I didn't know. I was pushed towards the building and told to wait outside. A soldier was left to guard me. The others went inside. I sat down in the sand, too hot and tired to make sense of what was going on.

An hour or so later, a convoy of armed trucks pulled up. A soldier came out the building and ushered me over to one of the vehicles. Guns pointed out every window. I tried to push away the images of being held hostage in a remote part of the Egyptian desert.

As we once again sped through the desert I stared into the wavering horizon, waiting for some sort of sign that my journey was near its end. I soon lost track of time. Suddenly the convoy turned off the sandy track and onto a proper road. We were approaching a populated area. Hurgada?! We pulled up outside a guest house on the periphery of the town. 'What's going on?', I asked again. The driver never replied. He went to speak to the owner of the guesthouse. then returned and signalled for me to get down from the truck. The convoy left as quickly as it had arrived. The guesthouse owner, a large jolly man, came out to greet me. 'Welcome friend!' he shouted. I grinned back, feeling a little confused at the sudden change in my situation.

The owner explained what had happened. Four policemen had been shot by militants in Qena - which was where our bus had been searched by the Egyptian army. When passing soldiers had discovered our bus broken down in the desert later, they had taken me to the nearest base for safety. From there, the army organised an armed convoy to escort me to Hurgada. I suddenly felt very grateful to the soldiers who rescued me!

A Travel Story in Poems
by Madeline Sharples

We went on Safari in the fall of 2013.

Preparing to Go
Even while I am on the elliptical
reading my New Yorker I wonder:
should I add more shirts?
should I pick out some silver jewelry?
do I need a pair of high heels?
While my Pilates trainer
says my form is excellent,
I visualize the piles of shirts, pants,
undies, jackets on the sofa,
shoes scattered on the floor,
and stuff bought
especially for this Kenya and Tanzania trip:
insect repellent, bite itch eraser,
and a new camera
with built in telescopic lens.
Even while I do my last stretches
I know I have more to do:
put my toiletries in travel containers,
get out my contact lens solutions,
lay out my travel clothes.
At least I distributed
my vitamins into separate baggies,
picked everything up at the cleaner,
and finished the last load of laundry.
Yet still weighing on my mind is
how much everything weighs.
Will we be able to board
those small planes in Africa
at or under the allowed poundage –
a measly thirty-three pounds?

Boni

A young person greets us at the airport
in a light blue and red dress
and hair in long tight braids
tied at the back of his neck.
So many beads in primary colors
adorn his head, neck, wrists, and fingers,
at first I think he is a girl.
No, he is our driver
in Kenya's Samburu district.
Boni is also a tracker.
He looks for footprints
on the bumpy red dirt roads
and fresh dung that indicates
which animals last visited.
Every once in a while
he takes out his monocular
to check in and under the trees,
and relies on his short-wave radio
for sighting news from other safari drivers.
When one spots elephant
or giraffe family,
about twenty drivers race
their Safari clients over
to click and gawk.

First Cheetah

The Cheetah sits
on its haunches
in the leafy shelter
of a fallen tree.
Thin black streaks like tears
line both sides of his mouth
While his large mournful eyes
with bright yellow centers
rimmed with orange
lookout for prey.
He turns his head
back and forth,

29

glancing quickly past us.
We are not what he wants for supper.

Herds and Prides
The cold pouring rain
does not stop the herds
of zebra, wildebeests, and other antelopes
– hartebeests, gazelles, topi,
tiny dik-dik, oryx, and impala
running gracefully and effectively
to escape our busy camera.
But the prize was the pride of five lions.
It didn't matter that the cigar smoking braggart
informed us this evening
he saw 51 unique lions today,
making light of our success.

Masai Mara Cultural Center
Benson greets us outside the fence
in a red dress and beads
around his waist, neck and arms.
$20 please, he said, for each,
then led us in to share
a bit of his culture with us.
The children in western attire
the older folks in full regalia
sang and danced, and
put beads on us so we could join in.
Later we stepped inside a mud house
with a simmering fire on the floor.
In the kitchen area flanked by two beds
I wondered how this family could breathe.
But this home owner is so proud
of her space: low benches, a row of pots and pans
and two hard sleeping mats,
she latched the door
and locked it with a padlock when we left.

Migration

Zebra and wildebeest
march toward the Mara River
for their biannual crossing
in their quest for more water.
Hundreds of them come in long straight lines.
And as they get to water's edge
they stop, look.
A few take the chance
and swim to the other side,
outracing the waiting crocodiles.
The others discuss
in shriek-y honks about when
and at which point to go.
Even though they don't speak
the same language
heads nod in agreement
as they walk en masse in one direction
then to the other,
deciding which is the safest spot
to outwit the crocs
getting ready for their dinner.
A few zebras,
the nominal leaders,
step toward water's edge.
They turn, they walk back and forth,
back and forth, and the others follow.
They return to starting point one
and outmaneuver the crocs again.

On the Savannah

Few trees populate this dry pale
land mass, called the Savannah.
The bumps we bounce upon
aren't roads
just trails made by wheels
digging into the porous ground.
Wildebeests scamper
across our path as we approach,
in our safari jeep.

31

The winds and rain
blow in as we
look from side to side
for animals, birds, termite mounds.
All safari roads are not alike
yet, they all lead us
to beauty, beasts, and
a chance sighting
of a mother rhino and her calf.

Lions in the Tree
We found four docile lions
in a little dell
high up on the tree
so relaxed to pay us any heed.
They looked like they didn't have
a care in the world.
Or had they just come back
from a kill,
exhausted from tearing
their prey apart,
eating their fill, and leaving
the rest to the vultures.
No wonder they looked content.
They've done their day's work,
and all that is left
is a big long nap.

Last Day
I'm satisfied
on this last day of Safari.
I've seen more animals and birds
than I ever dreamed of – more
than Noah could ever board in his ark.
The geography varied
in each place we visited
from bumpy hills
with bare trees in Samburu,
a vast plain with little vegetation

called the Savannah in the Masai Mara,
rolling greens covered with dense rocks
and thunderstorms every evening on the Serengeti,
dust and hot dry air in Lake Manyara,
and now at our last place, Ngorongoro,
windblown red dusty soil covers
me inside and out.

Boni

Words of Magic
by Ronald Mackay

"Please!" The sari-clad women graciously appeal to me to lead the way. Night has fallen on Tamil Nadu. I can barely distinguish the path leading into dim undergrowth.

Why me? They're the farmers. It's their land, their millet. The granary belongs to the village. I smile and gesture to an older woman.

"She is suggesting you go first, Dr. Mackay," says Abhay.

"Me?"

"You're wearing boots," says Chandresh.

I compare my Australian Redbacks to the women's bare feet, but still fail to understand.

"It's dark," says Abhay.

"They seek the residual heat on the bare path," says Chandresh.

"The snakes," explains Abhay.

Now I understand. My boots offer some protection if I trample one.

Since daybreak, our driver from the Swaminathan Foundation in Chennai, has driven agronomists Abhay and Chandresh, and me as the evaluation specialist, from one isolated hamlet to another, in the monsoon-soaked Jawadhu Hills. In each, barefoot farmers, all women, have greeted us with smiles and fruit drinks, clasping their hands and inclining their heads to respect the sacred in us. I've learned to return the honour.

Women have led me to the village granary where they store their harvested millet, an earthenware pot for each variety. My task is to confirm the volume of each variety harvested. The Swaminathan Foundation propagated the seed they've planted. The European Union has paid for its free distribution. This joint project seeks to reinvigorate the cultivation of high-quality millet in Tamil Nadu.

If villagers resume eating this traditional grain, their health and the general wellbeing of the hamlets in the Jawadhu Hills will improve. Farmers can sell their surplus and with the money, send their daughters to school. All will benefit. This is how development works.

It takes an evaluation specialist to ensure that money granted for development by governments and charities, has been used as intended. The specialist also determines to what extent the goals of the project are being met. For this project, it falls to me to visit the hamlets and their farmers, to gather the appropriate evidence, to assess how well the project is faring. Finally, I will suggest ways to get better results. The European Union will use my report to determine precisely what taxpayers are getting for their investment in assisting poor farmers to grow, consume and sell more millet.

"Make much noise as you go. Snakes will be slithering away before you are getting close," Abhay says.

My Redbacks protect only my feet and ankles. Fears spring to mind. Snakes? What kind? How big? How aggressive? Venomous? Might they strike at ankle level? Higher? Will they give any warning?

"Be making a noise," Chandresh repeated.

I understand now, why neither he nor Abhay have visited any of the granaries today. Verification is, I know, my job. But has fear played any part in their reluctance?

All five women are smiling, waiting for me to lead. Surely, they won't knowingly place me in danger. I smile at them, peer into the lush undergrowth and step out bravely.

What kind of noise should I make? Shout? Whistle? Tramp loudly? Why not recite verses of poetry to help distract my mind from any danger?

I begin to recite in the dialect of my Scottish youth. My five farmers follow closely.

Ae day, an ae nicht
A yowden druft fae the cauld nor-east
Has whussilt and pufft and blawn the craa's aoot the luft
Blatterin' sairly.
Hit reeshlit the wuids and gart them shuft
Like a breer o barley.

Rustlings in the undergrowth give me no clue as to their origin.

The granary is typical of those I've inspected in daylight, the size of a small garden shed with a thatched roof. Five stones support each corner to raise the granary three feet above the ground. Each third stone is flatter, thinner and much larger than those above and below. They serve the same purpose that rat-guards serve on boat-lines -- to keep pilfering rodents out. As additional precaution and shelter from rain, the grain inside is stored in covered clay pots like the amphorae the Greeks use for olive oil.

So far, so good. In the tiny interior, I check the volumes of each variety that these farmers have grown, harvested and stored to feed the families in their hamlet, educate their daughters. They clap, delighted, when my moon-lit observations confirm the varieties and volumes that they themselves have recorded.

Now for the return trip. Surely no snake can be dumb enough to slither back onto the trail so soon after twelve feet have tramped past?

Back we head, me in the lead. Douglas Young's words loud and clear to warn wayward reptiles and to bolster my confidence.

The cypress busses is aa blaan crookit;
The green's are as clorty as only doo-cot;
The wind-faan aiples'll hae te be cuikit afore they get waar;
The plooms are aa wersh they're that sair drookit and clortied wi glaur.

Not a single snake!

The villagers offer blossoms and petals in Hindu ceremony in thanks.

We clasp hands and bow our departure, but the older woman clutches my arm.

"She is begging you," says Chandresh, "'please teach us the words.'"

"Words?"

"Of the spell," says Abhay.

"The one they say you used to ward off the snakes," adds Chandresh. "They want to learn the words, so they'll never again be afraid to walk the path at night."

The women shake their heads, meaning, 'Please!'.

Soon, all these sari-clad farmers have committed the words of Douglas Young's *Fife Equinox* to memory. A polyglot himself, he would have been proud of them. Perhaps of me to!

So, the next time you happen to find yourself in the Jawadhu Hills of Tamil Nadu after sunset, don't be surprised if you hear my Scottish dialect gently chanted by a single line of women making their way back to the hamlet from the communal granary where they store their millet.

36

Teetering on the Edge
by Robyn Boswell

By the time we reached Dubrovnik our bus had already broken down a few times, but after all we were on a budget camping trip. The camping ground we were supposed to stay in was closed for some unknown reason, but apparently that was no surprise, so we ended up a little way past Dubrovnik in a gorgeous camp right on the edge of the Adriatic Sea. We spent a day wandering the magnificent, ancient walls of Dubrovnik, blissfully unaware of how they would be battered and shattered in the yet to come war.

After a couple of day's break swimming in the warm sea and generally taking a breather, we had the tents down and loaded early, ready to enjoy the majesty of the coast road to Split, supposedly one of the most beautiful drives in the world. We settled in for a long day with 'The Horse with No Name' blasting away on the bus's speakers. Our courier, Bill, always played it when we had an early start and I can never hear that song without being carried back to the carefree days of our European wanderings. We wound our way along the narrow road, which was carved out of the steep coastal hillside. Those of us on the left looked way down to the clear blue depths of the ocean. Quite disconcerting if you didn't like heights!

Not far into the journey, we were about to tackle a sharp a right-hand bend when there was a sudden jerk as the bus kept going straight ahead, then ground to a halt. There was dead silence as we all looked at each other and even our driver, Tony, sat stone-still for a few moments. The steering rod had broken, giving him no control, but fortunately his skill had saved us from an almost inevitable fate. There we were, stuck half-way across a busy road with very little between us and the cliffs plunging down to the sea. We clambered off the bus and it was then we realised just how lucky we were. The very front of the bus was overhanging the cliff. Another few seconds and we would have tumbled to our doom. With so little room to shelter, we ended up sitting on the side of the road with our feet on the edge of the cliff whilst seemingly maniacal drivers sped past.

Fearing for our lives, some of our group unloaded and unfurled their red sleeping bags and went round both sides of the corner to wave them to warn oncoming traffic. That tactic was only moderately successful. One driver pulled a knife on them, others saw it as an opportunity to speed up and show their machismo. Meantime, the rest of us teetered on the edge, much like the bus.

Tony and Bill managed to hitchhike back to the camp and borrow another bus to rescue us and we ended up back in the beautiful camp by the ocean, while they had to deal with the nightmare of saving a crippled bus on a crowded road with mad drivers.

There wasn't a lot we could do over the next few days, but enjoy basking in the sun, drinking cheap booze in the camp bar and swimming in the crystal-clear ocean. We dived off the low cliffs and climbed back up ladders embedded in the rocks, taking care not to impale ourselves on the nasty spikes of the sea urchins clinging to the rocks just below the surface. Some people found out just how painful that could be.

We were party to at least some of the panic going on behind the scenes. They were going to buy a bus; it was high season in Europe; there were no buses; they hired a bus from Munich; the bus got just out of Munich and the motor blew up. Some of our group found this too much to take. At a camp meeting, strong opinions were aired and tempers frayed. Some people decided to hitchhike north and meet us in Vienna. We wondered if we'd ever see them again. My friends and I were happy to hang around until something happened. The famous New Zealand saying, "She'll be right, mate", was our mantra.

Eventually a mechanic and his girlfriend were dispatched in a van from England with the necessary spare parts. They drove non-stop for three days and three nights and at 3.00 one afternoon we were finally given the order to break camp as we'd be going non-stop to Vienna, more than 1000kms away.

Unfortunately for Helen and I we'd been rostered on cooking duty that night and there wasn't going to be anywhere to stop to buy a meal. We got supplies in a small village – all we could find were canned frankfurters and beans and a few veggies. We probably bought several year's supply; it must have been very puzzling to the shopkeepers. At dusk we pulled off the side of the road in the stunning mountains, unloaded the gas cookers and scrambled together a not very popular frankfurter stew.

So much for the magnificent views we had been promised. We traversed the whole coast in the middle of the night, waking in the morning for breakfast at a roadside service centre that could have been anywhere. Apart from necessary comfort stops – sometimes we had to perch under trees in the forest – and the border, we were driven on and on, swapping drivers from time to time, until finally, late in the afternoon we pulled into our camp in Vienna. To our surprise all of the hitch-hikers were waiting for us and they certainly had their own tales of adventure to share.

I'd like to say that that was the end of the troubles with the bus, but unfortunately it was to dog us all the way back to England. The vision of 48 people pushing a bus from Germany to Liechtenstein is one I will never forget!

Canberra, In A Roundabout Way
by Mike Cavanagh

My family headed off in the autumn school holidays of 1963 in Dad's 1959 black Chrysler Royal. The car was my father's pride and joy; chrome bumpers, full body-length chrome side stripes, white rear wing tips, white-walled tyres and push button automatic transmission. She (of course a *she*) was such a smooth and classy ride we dubbed her 'Black Beauty'. We were on a three-day jaunt to see the nation's capital, Canberra, and on board with me (ten years old at that time) were my mum and dad (Ray and Lou), and my brother Peter, who was two years older than me. Now, for all those readers who've never been to Canberra, a few things need to be explained.

First off, Canberra was founded by and for politicians. All Australians are born with a healthy disrespect for 'pollies', and even Australian politicians themselves start out this way, until they are lured to the 'dark side' by already fallen 'darksiders'. To 'take the micky' out of politicians is almost a national pastime and is possibly only matched by bagging out lawyers. On the other hand, teachers, doctors and nurses are sacrosanct; lawyers and politicians only just scramble a half a rung above The All Blacks. Moving on – can't even talk about *them*!

Second thing to note: Canberra is a designed city. Designed by an architect whose design was chosen by politicians from amongst many other submitted plans. Now, on paper, and you can see this effect if you view Canberra's street map in Google maps or similar, the street design for the main centre ('Civic') and the southern section ('Parliamentary Circle') across a lake looks quite interesting, almost *avant garde*. In fact, it harks back to Plato's most perfect geometric shape, the sphere, which translated into two dimensions is circles. Lots of circles. Pretty, pretty. Until you get into a car and drive.

Human evolution has well trained the human brain to (i) see, (ii) react and (iii) accomplish, in this order as efficiently as possible. See red fruit? Swing over to red fruit. Grab and eat red fruit. See beautiful cave woman? Walk over to beautiful cave woman. Produce large club and do what comes naturally. I suspect the Neanderthals would have died out much sooner if they'd all been living in Canberra.

So, getting around and through Canberra involves a great deal of going around and around. For anyone who has a follow your nose sense of direction, this is a nightmare. Heading south? Easy, it's that way... er, it *was* that way as you watch it swing from ahead to over our left shoulder, then behind you … er why are we now heading north? Oh wait, here it comes again… and goes again…

If at any time you notice you are running out of petrol, oh dear. If you can even glimpse a petrol station driving through Canberra, don't go there, it's a mirage. In their wisdom, the kindly fore-fathers (politicians!) decided things as ugly and plebeian as service stations should be kept well out of sight and away from the main roads; don't want the money wielding tourists thinking Canberra was for the masses. Oh, my goodness gracious, no! What's more, let's not even draw attention to them by having signs pointing in their direction. Excellent!

So, this being our first visit to Canberra, no surprise that we couldn't find the Acadia Motel we'd booked into, which was supposedly close in to the Parliamentary Circle, the southern part of the city. After taking half an hour simply to find the bridge and cross over from the north, we were now locked into 'veer left' like a dodgem car going round anti-clockwise all its life.

On the way down, we'd stopped for a comfort stop before getting to Canberra, which was to our great good fortune as public toilets are about as hard to find as petrol stations. Mum had allowed Pete to get into the front beside Dad while she sat in the back with me, so Dad got Pete to investigate the one small scale street map we had and identify the street the Acadia Motel was on. Some five minutes later, and four complete 'turn map upside down' events, Pete said,

"Wandsworth Avenue, Dad. We need Wandsworth Avenue!"

"Good work, Peter! OK, everyone, keep looking for 'Wandsworth Avenue' and call out as soon as you see it.

Then a bit later, "No Wandsworth Avenue yet? Anyone?"

"No Dad."

Mum, knowing geographical directions were not her strong suit, took to making little commentaries about interesting things we were passing.

"Oh look, there's the consulate for Brazil! What a lovely flag they have."

Dad: "Any sign yet, boys?" having accepted that the 'boys' were going to be the only ones actually looking.

"No, Dad." We replied in chorus.

"Oh look," Mum continued on her merry daydreaming come-tourist blub, "There's the German Consulate. Isn't it strange that it's so close to the Polish one?"

Her wit was lost on us entirely.

"Come on boys, we must be near it!"

"Sorry Dad!" "Not yet Dad!"

"Oh look, there are birds bathing in the lovely fountain in front of the Acadia Motel. I think they're lorikeets." Mum burbled on.

"What's this street boys, is this the one?"

"No Dad – this is Fraser Avenue." I replied, puffing my chest out that I'd identified it and told Dad before my brother could. Then,

"What? Mum? What did you just say?" Pete swivelled around in the front and looked at mum.

"Sorry Peter, what did you ask?"

"Mum, did you just say the Acadia Motel?"

"Yes. Why? Oh!"

"Mum!" kids in chorus with Dad's "Lou!"

We had to drive around for another ten minutes to get back to the driveway. When we went past the fountain, we noted that the birds were indeed lorikeets.

My mum might not have been real hot with directions, but she sure knew her birds.

Black Beauty

"Being Seen"
by Nancy McBride

Twice I've opened the Boston Globe—not a regular reader—and been literally transported, each big time. First, when I lived in Buffalo, someone thrust a copy in my face, and said, "Go, East!" It was kismet. I spotted a blind ad describing a job in Massachusetts—no company name, only a post box number. That job quickly materialized, and the girls and I shifted our lives East five weeks later.

The second time, it magically opened to a full-page ad for Northwest Airlines! They were starting flights from Boston to Sydney, and the maiden flight was $724 RT. A single mother, knowing I'd never be able to pay full fare, I booked immediately, and got THE last ticket to go 5 weeks hence.

TRIP PREP

1. Call Nigel, a man I'd met at breakfast at a B&B in Edinburgh, Scotland, and with whom I had exchanged business cards. "Please meet me at the airport, take me to my hostel, and be an emergency contact for my girls? Okay?" "Certainly!" Check.

2. Call my friend, Chere for contacts. (She was a sophisticated woman who once wore her floor length mink coat and a swoopy hat to support me singing in a local concert. Both the chorus and the audience gasped then froze as she made her dramatic entrance—late—swishing down the isle to flop flamboyantly in the first row. Shook, we started the concert over "from the top!" An Australian billionaire's wife, here she was living with a local Italian she'd met skiing in the Alps. Apparently, her husband sent her anywhere she wanted to go when she was bored. He thought she was going to nursing school. Far be it for me...) Check.

3. Pack in a large backpack:
Hooded jacket, scarf, mittens, fleece vest, jeans, black turtleneck, long black, knit skirt, scoop neck black top, nighty, bathroom stuff, camera, sketchbook, hiking boots, socks, undies, dangly earrings, tickets and traveler's checks. Check.

4. Itinerary. Nope. No plans whatsoever. Check.

5. Contact list with phone numbers. I had Chere's best friends' and her husband's. She had told them each to be good to me and told me not to tell them what she was doing, except going to nursing school. Check.

The first of my two weeks it poured. I was in a Hostel at Bondi Beach, and ended up helping an artist hang his show in a gallery alongside the beach shops, getting me out of the rain. The artist asked me to the opening. I asked my friend, Nigel, to go with me. "No one gets invited to those openings! Only the big shots!" "Well, then, I guess you're now a big shot!"

One rainy day I watched men surfing. Suddenly, they came flying out of the water, clamoring up the beach screaming, "Shark!" "Shark!" They had mistakenly thought dolphins that'd joined them catching waves, were sharks. Once they realized they weren't, they scuttled back in and surfed with them. It was magical.

Finally sunny, while on a tour bus to the nearby canyons, I was unceremoniously dumped on the outskirts of Sydney because they had Japanese tour company reps that wanted to go, and there wasn't room. Three of us, tossed and flummoxed, righted ourselves, then rented an Ugly Duckling car and made up our own 18-hour tour. Wonderful locals fed us and showed us around. It was delightful.

Eating supper in the hostel one evening, I pondered aloud, "Should I go to Melbourne and visit Chere's husband, or not?" My pals shrugged, "Why not?" I called Ian, and he said they'd love to have me! His swanky, aloof daughters picked me up from the airport. Surprise! No guest room in the inn; I was shown to a dressing room off Ian's bedroom where Chere's furs were kept—actually a closet. I slept on the fainting couch. I shared his bathroom with a sunken tub, and gold fixtures. This mansion was a not-so miniature Versailles, with three monstrous bedrooms, each with bathrooms the size of my downstairs! It was pure luxury with a massive foyer, terrazzo flooring, ceiling murals, manicured gardens, a formal dining room for 30, Ming vases, and some Impressionists paintings—real ones. And it echoed with loneliness.

Ian and I cooked supper, and we four ate in the kitchen. After dinner, he asked if we could have a "family night" to sort Chere's society press-clippings for scrapbooks. The girls—Paris Hilton types—rolled their eyes and excused themselves. Poor, lonely guy; I said I'd help. At four in the morning we quit. We had sorted at least five boxes of articles about her high society life that he'd meticulously clipped practically every day of their lives together. She had been a young, famous fashion model—eye candy—when he, the rich, up-and-coming middle-aged mogul married her. He went back to work, and she was coiffed, tucked, photographed, and bored.

One afternoon, her friend took me out. She introduced me to all her fancy friends as Chere's best friend from the States, a "famous" food editor, author, etc. At first, I checked over my shoulder, looking for whomever, then figured out it was *me*, and gushed, "Oh! SO, nice to meet you." (Gag.) Her tucked plastic surgeon was my favorite. Pathetic.

Later, her young lawyer lover (not her husband) picked us up in a limousine to take us to dinner. They politely asked where I'd like to go, but I deferred, not having a clue where I was, nor what part I played in this Fellini film. Openly, they conferred, "Well, where can we be SEEN?" I had to pretend to gaze, disinterested, out the window, sipping my champagne, pinky extended. It was all I COULD do in those circumstances.

We went to the *right* restaurant, tipped the concierge heavily (and not subtly), and were shown to the *right* table, where we were "SEEN" by the elite of Melbourne. "So! YOU'RE Chere's American friend? How IS she?"

I have now beeeen seen.

Poor Economy
by Frank Kusy

I can't remember where I saw the advert for the Economy bus to Athens. All that I can remember was that it was ridiculously cheap.

The booking company was called Economy Holidays, and it was run by the appropriately named Mr Economous. His brochure – which featured a picture of the corpulent Greek – promised to get me to Athens in 36 hours. In fact, it took nearly five days.

The reason it took that long was that Mr Economous was a crook. Things started out okay – the bus reached Dover with no trouble, and a smooth crossing by hovercraft to Calais put all 40 passengers in an optimistic frame of mind. Then matters deteriorated.

'Where's the bus?' said Roger, our party leader.

'What bus?' we chorused.

'The connecting bus to take us on through Europe!'

We stared around us. The coach terminal at Calais harbour was empty.

'I'll get on the blower,' said Roger, scratching his head. 'There's got to be a reason for this.'

The next day, having returned to Dover, we learnt the reason: Mr Economous had absconded with all his company's funds and was being chased up the M1 motorway by the highway police. While we awaited the arrival of a *Daily Mirror* reporter to publicise our plight, eight more people got fed up of waiting and returned to their homes.

Around noon, Roger had some heartening news. 'The police have tracked down Mr Economous!' he told us. 'They found him eating some sandwiches in a lay-by near Bristol and have hauled him back to London!'

'So, are we still going to Athens?' I asked sceptically.

'Oh, yes,' beamed Roger. 'They've promised us a coach!' He wasn't beaming long. Six hours later, having returned to Calais, a coach was sighted. Unfortunately, as it weaved its way dangerously towards us, it became apparent that the driver was drunk.

'I sorry I late,' slurred the balding Pole out of the window. 'I stop for the vodka.'

Roger was a big man. And he was definitely not out of shape. Moments after the bus came to a halt – only a foot away from the edge of the harbour – he reached into the driver's cab, dragged the occupant out of it, and beat him to a pulp.

'That was a bit drastic,' I commented. 'Couldn't you have waited till he sobered up?'

Roger blew on his knuckles. 'Not really,' he said grimly. 'That bus was missing a wheel and the fuel tank had a bad leak in it.'

On the third day, back in Dover, four of us made a flying visit to Mr Economous's London office – with a phalanx of journalists and police in tow – and demanded another bus. And to our great surprise, back in Calais, another bus did turn up: this time with all wheels intact and a sober driver.

The driver may have been sober, but he had no idea where he was going. We proceeded around Austria in circles for a further day until he was forced to buy a road map from a ramshackle gas station on the outskirts of Villach. Two of our company wandered off to buy some chocolate and never reappeared. I often wonder what became of them.

Getting to Athens proved the best part of the holiday. By the time we arrived, on the evening of day five, the 13 remaining passengers had formed strong bonds of friendship. The rest of the trip, perhaps inevitably, was a bit of an anti-climax: we toured the sights of the city together, we took a boat trip to Poros together, and we took a lacklustre trip to Delphi together.

It was a pity about Delphi. I had read so much about the famous oracle there and had been dying to ask it a question.

'Here, see!' said our guide as he took us to the ruined temple to Apollo. 'Here priests inhale fumes like ethane from fissure in rock and fall into ecstatic trancing!'

I looked around. There wasn't a fume in sight.

'Where is fumes?' I asked the small, grinning guide. 'I want to have trancing!'

He giggled and held a smouldering cigarette to the rock. 'There is fumes!'

While the rest of the group moved on, I found a toppled temple column and sat down on one of its large granite rings.

Then, when I was sure nobody else was looking, I tried to commune with Apollo.

'Oh, great god Apollo,' I wedged my eyelids shut. 'I know you don't exist, but just in case you do, tell me please, what does the future hold for me?'

There was a long silence. So long that I feared I had not been heard.

Then Apollo spoke. 'Hey, mister!' He said. 'Is that man-made?'

I opened my eyes to be confronted by a large, smiling American.

'What?' I said.

'That ring-a-ding thing you're sitting on. Is that man-made?'

One last event remained to be crossed off our party's Grecian bucket list – the famous Daphne Wine Festival.

'Blimey, only 50 drachmas (2 dollars) for as much as you can drink!' I announced on arrival. 'And look, they've got about 60 barrels of local wines to choose from!'

I'll never know how I got back to my guest house in Athens that night. All that I knew was that I woke up next morning – on the roof, in my sleeping bag – with the sun beating down on my unprotected face and flies in vast numbers buzzing around my head.

'Oh...my...God,' I slowly intoned to myself,

'This...is...the...worst...hangover...of...my...life.'

Then I compounded my pain. Automatically reaching for my water bottle, I lifted it to my parched mouth in the full expectation of cool, rehydrating H2O. What I got instead was a glug of sour, dehydrating Retsina which I forgot I'd smuggled out of the festival.

As my stomach rebelled and I struggled to get my head out of the sleeping bag, I made one silent determination: I was *never* going to drink wine again!

The market in Dajabon
by Lindsay de Feliz

Friends from Canada visited me in the Dominican Republic and they wanted to go on a road trip. They wanted to go to the market at Dajabon, which is the border crossing to Haiti in the north west of the country and holds a massive weekly market when Haitians cross into the DR for the day to sell their wares. It was not on my bucket list but one of the advantages of visitors is that they make you do things. I checked Google maps which stated 76.4 kilometres and one hour and 14 minutes. Fine I thought. Unfortunately, I did not realise that in the same way that a Dominican minute is not the same as an English minute, a Dominican kilometre is much longer than an English kilometre.

We set off in my 30-year-old jeep, with no air conditioning, no central locking, and everything is manual including the cassette player, bumping and bouncing our way down the road, accompanied by constant squeaking from the failing suspension.

After only 30 minutes, the front offside tyre exploded and we shuddered to a halt. I have no jack, but being the Dominican Republic, it doesn't matter, as within seconds a man driving a bleach truck stopped. You buy bleach from the tank on the back. He got out his jack and within minutes the tyre was changed. Impressive that his yellow underpants matched his truck.

We set off again, bumping and bouncing a tad less and eventually reached Sabaneta where we bought a new tyre and asked how much further it was to Dajabon. One chap said 40 minutes, but only 30 if you drove slowly! Another said an hour and a half. The closer we got to Dajabon the cars were increasingly replaced by beautiful floppy eared cows.

Eventually we hit Dajabon after three and a half hours and 150 kilometres. So much for Google maps. Following a much-needed toilet and lunch stop, we went to find the market. Somehow, we arrived at the border post which looked suitably official and even a tad scary, so we turned around and ended up in a dusty field which I assume was a car park near the border crossing.

There were no cars there, but I parked the jeep and we clambered out to look over the simple fence, only a couple of feet high, which was the border with Haiti.

As we walked towards the fence a solitary soldier, clutching his dangerous looking rifle, watched us closely, and I smiled and waved. The greeting was not returned.

We walked up to the fence and there beyond it was the Massacre River, named as it was where thirty French buccaneers were killed by Spanish settlers in 1728. The river looked shallow, with mud banks and was full of naked men bathing and women washing clothes. Sheets, towels and brightly coloured clothes were strewn over the banks on the far side and beyond there was nothing, just a sense of desolation. This was another country. This was Haiti and I was six inches away from it.

A small boy in the river tried to scramble up the mud bank towards us as we stood, open mouthed looking into what appeared to be hell on earth. He was followed by other tiny kids trying to swim and stagger through the muddy, filthy water towards us.

"Dame 5 pesos," he demanded unsmiling, looking up at me with big brown eyes and a snotty nose. Of course I would give him 5 pesos, but as I reached into my bag noticing the hope and gratitude in his eyes, the Dominican soldier approached me, his gun no longer slung across his body but pointing at me. He signalled at me to move back.

"I'll just give this kid some money," I said to him in Spanish. "Non," he replied and came closer waving his gun at me menacingly.

I had no choice and took one last heart wrenching look at the desolation, deflation, disappointment and despair in those large brown eyes, as a single tear coursed down his grubby little check.

We walked back to the car in silence, deep in thought and drove towards the market, keeping the windows closed in case someone reached in, dripping with sweat, inching slowly through crowds of people, cars, trucks and bikes before eventually managing to find somewhere to park.

The market was enormous, part outside and a massive blue building with stalls inside, upstairs and down. The first thing to hit you is the smell of sweaty bodies. The stink was appalling, and it was very hot, very crowded, dusty and crazy. People were rushing everywhere. Women with bags and containers on their heads yelling what they were selling. Men rushing hither and thither with wheelbarrows, empty and full.

"How long do you want to stay," I shouted to my Canadian friends.

"Oh my God it is awful. Ten minutes maybe?"

It seemed like an awfully long way to go for 10 minutes, but I was in total agreement. We went into the inside market where it was somewhat cooler and less pungent. There were clothes, shoes, bags, electrical goods, food household goods, cleaning materials, apparently all at good prices, although we didn't pause to check. We just wanted to get out of there.

People were eating, sleeping, lying on piles of rugs and blankets and I bought a bag of hot chillis for 20 pesos, and that was all we bought.

Arriving home, my little self-appointed bodyguard, a local boy called Chivirico, had been watching out for us and ran to open the gate. He was the same age as the child in the river, but he had a worthwhile life in front of him, he had hope, food, clothes and a chance of a future.

I cooked an Indian curry with the chillis. They were the hottest I have ever eaten. The market at Dajabon had its revenge.

Tyre change

Lost in Translation
by Rob Johnson

One of the most daunting obstacles that my wife Penny and I had to overcome when we moved from the UK to Greece fourteen years ago was learning the language. We'd done our best with a variety of books and CDs for months in advance, but we soon discovered that there all kinds of traps for the linguistically unwary.

In particular, there are many examples in Greek where two words are spelt exactly the same but mean something entirely different, depending on which syllable is stressed. This can lead to some highly embarrassing – and sometimes downright dangerous – situations if you happen to put the stress in the wrong place. For instance, the word for glass is *tzámi* (TZA-mee) and the word for mosque is *tzamí* (tza-MEE), which could have proved a little awkward when we needed to order a replacement for a broken window in our camper van.

Similarly, there are many pairs of words that are remarkably similar, such as *domáta* (tomato) and *domátio* (room), and also *kounávi* (pine marten) and *kouniáda* (sister-in-law). Unless you're very careful, therefore, you could easily find yourself phoning a hotel and asking for "a double tomato for my wife and I, and a separate tomato for my pine marten." Somehow, I think you'd be told that the hotel was booked solid for the next several months.

Besides having to be careful with your pronunciation in Greece, you also need to be wary of using slang or idioms when talking to an English-speaking Greek, regardless of how fluent they might be. Since I'd previously taught English as a foreign language, this was something that wasn't at all new to me. Penny, on the other hand, had had no such background, and I often found myself having to "translate" some of her more obscure words and phrases such as "That's a different kettle of fish altogether" and "It all went a bit pear-shaped". She wasn't entirely happy about my frequently correcting her, but she did get her revenge one day when I inadvertently used an expression that plenty of native English speakers probably wouldn't even know.

The gaffe happened when we were talking to a guy called Dionysis, who runs our local olive press. We'd been telling him that we were just about to go back to the UK for a week or two and we were desperately trying to get everything sorted out on the land before we left.

'One of the biggest jobs is getting all the grass cut,' I said.

'Yes,' said Dionysis, 'and at this time of year, it keeps growing back again as soon as you've cut it.'

'Exactly,' I said. 'So, with 20,000 square metres [5 acres], you have to start all over again as soon as you've finished. It's like painting the Forth Road Bridge.'

I knew it was a mistake the moment the words were out of my mouth, and Penny shot me a look which could only be interpreted as "Oh yes, Mr English Teacher, and I thought we weren't supposed to use that sort of language."

But it was too late. The simile was already out of the bag, and Dionysis pounced on it before I had a chance to explain.

'So you have your own bridge in England, do you?' he said, clearly but erroneously impressed.

'No, not at all. It's just an expression which means that—'

'And that is why you're going back to England? To paint this bridge of yours?'

To Penny's obvious amusement, I floundered to come up with an explanation of what the phrase means, and eventually Dionysis seemed to understand. Or so I thought.

After we'd come back from the UK, Dionysis and his family invited us to their traditional Easter Sunday celebrations, and after lunch, I was sitting having a drink with Dionysis and some of his brothers-in-law (he has several) when he suddenly announced, 'Robert has his own bridge in England, you know.'

Five pairs of eyes popped in surprise.

'No, no,' I began, but Dionysis was warming to his theme.

'Yes,' he said, 'and he had to go back to England recently to paint it.'

I tried to interject and disabuse Dionysis and his brothers-in-law of the idea that Penny and I must be incredibly wealthy if we could afford to own an entire bridge, but by now, the floodgates were open, and I was bombarded with questions.

'So how big *is* this bridge?' asked one brother-in-law.

'Well, it's about two and a half kilometres long, I think, but we don't actually—'

'Wow,' said another brother-in-law. 'That's nearly as big as the Rio Bridge.'

'Yes, but—'

'How many litres of paint do you need?'

'The thing is, you see, we—'

'What colour do you paint it?'

'No, you don't underst—'

'Do you do all the work yourselves or do you have help?'

As if my awkward embarrassment couldn't have got any more acute, Dionysis then threw in that this was our "fourth" road bridge.

Eyes popped even wider.

'You have three other bridges?'

'But painting just one of them must be a never-ending job.'

I attempted to explain that this was pretty much the point of what I'd been trying to convey in the first place, but I was interrupted by one of the brothers-in-law insisting that everyone drink a toast to 'Robert and Penny's road bridges!'

Penny, of course, has never let me forget the Forth Road Bridge fiasco, and since then, I've never once dared to pick her up on her use of even the most obscure of English idioms. With what I consider to be one of the cruellest of ironies, though, I've since discovered that a far more durable paint has been developed which means that, in future, the Forth Road Bridge will only need to be repainted once in every twenty-five years. So, there's another stitch lost from the rich tapestry of the English language, albeit a potentially rather confusing one.

Mexican Apples
by Cat Jenkins

"No hay manzanas en Mexico," the old man growled.

No apples in Mexico? Was that really true? Maybe he just didn't like the question. Or maybe he just didn't like me.

He turned away, back bent under a large basket of avocados, muttering to himself. I caught the words "gringa" and "loca."

I'd been traveling all summer, trying to make the most of what I saw as my final break before entering the "real world" where I'd have to find a job and settle down to the business of being an adult, for once and for all, until death do I part. To tell the truth, I was a little reluctant and a little scared. So, I took off for Mexico as soon as graduation was over.

So far, it had been great. There had been some culture shock. I had learned that girls who get pinched in the market place aren't supposed to punch their admirers. I learned that if you bought anything, the vendors would ask you how much you "wanted" to pay on the receipt as opposed to how much you actually paid. This allowed you to bend some of the strictures about bringing merchandise over the border. I learned that you really, honestly shouldn't drink the water...or eat anything washed in the water, if you weren't acclimated to any local digestive bugaboos.

Now it was autumn and I was in Taxco. Drought ruled. There was no water in the cheap motel I'd taken. I spent the night sitting in my room's wide, adobe window frame, watching more stars than I ever thought the sky could hold. Somewhere a dog or coyote barked. There was an answer. And another. Soon a canine symphony was traveling from horizon to horizon, speaking a wild kind of joy.

Increasingly over the last couple of weeks I'd been having bouts of homesickness. Crouched on the windowsill, feeling dusty and grubby from lack of water to wash in, I thought of autumn at home.

Leaves would be every color found on the warm side of the rainbow. The air would be sharp with frost and scented pines. Everyone would be snuggled in sweaters pulled from summer storage, still smelling slightly of camphor. And there would be lovely things like pumpkin pie, hazelnuts fresh from the tree, and apples.

Wonderful apples.

I closed my eyes and relived walking through an orchard, picking a perfect fruit, biting into its tart, sweet, crunchiness.

Come morning, all I wanted was to taste a newly picked apple. So, I walked down the narrow streets of Taxco, naively thinking that there should be orchards in what I considered a rural locale.

That old man with the avocados made me mentally slap myself. I was thousands of miles away from where apples grew naturally. I drooped under my dashed hopes.

A small girl had witnessed the grumbling exchange. She tugged at the hem of my jacket and said, "Senorita, mi padre tiene manzanas."

"Your father has apples?"

She nodded enthusiastically. "Si. El los hace."

"He MAKES them?" I thought I must have misunderstood. With a wide, innocent smile, she grabbed my hand and pulled toward the road which led to the center of town. She chattered about how beautiful her father's apples were. I let her lead me, curious to see how this would turn out.

It seemed my exuberant, little guide was headed toward the town's main street.

We turned a corner and stepped into a river of silver. Taxco is known for its silversmiths. Apparently, this was the section of town devoted to the art. Both sides of the street were lined with tables, cases, booths displaying beautifully crafted silver. In the clear, mid-morning light jewelry, utensils and sculptures rippled and gleamed.

My little friend pulled my hand, impatient. Almost blinded by the reflection, I let her bring me to a stand halfway down the street. The man behind the makeshift counter gave me a huge smile.

"Eh, pequena, donde has estado?" he queried, "Little one, where have you been?"

His daughter answered that she had found a lady who was looking for apples and proudly pointed to her papa's display.

Silver apples as paperweights, serving dishes, Christmas ornaments, picture frames, belt buckles and every other creation that lent itself to this noble metal surrounded me. I laughed, crumbling in mirth until father and daughter exchanged significant glances. A crazy tourist was among them!

Finally, I did pick out a delicate necklace with tiny, silver apples strung on an elegant chain. I thanked the little girl for helping me find apples and walked up the street to the place where northbound buses stopped.

I'll never forget picking silver, Mexican apples. It was the day I finally decided to go home.

Flotel
by Syd Blackwell

Our 2015 Bolivia tour was incredible. One segment was four days on a floating hotel exploring the Ibare and Mamoré rivers, Amazon tributaries. We taxied from the airport at Trinidad to the broad, brown Ibare. Across the water was *Reina de Enín*, our flotel.

A boat zipped towards us with a male and female passenger and a scruffy driver. The smiling man bid goodbye to the young woman, while the boat driver loaded our bags. The woman was Christine, who had paid for a single day of cruising. The departing man was the owner of the boat. The scruffy guy was our captain, Alvaro.

We were shown to our room, the largest and most forward on the boat. Soon, Alvaro returned for a tour. Surprisingly, we learned we were the only guests on a boat with a capacity of thirty-six and a crew of four! First, we met Fabi, the cook, then Bambino, who was at the helm, and lastly, Ariel, a young man with a perpetual smile. *Reina de Enín* has four levels. The bottom is a catamaran. Everything above is the original boat, lifted by crane and attached to the catamaran base. The lowest deck has guest rooms. The next deck, dining room, kitchen and crew rooms. On the top, the wheelhouse, hammock area and rear viewing deck. We just knew we were going to be treated royally.

As soon as we were moving, we went to lunch. Fabi presented *surubi*, an Amazon fish, beef cooked in tomatoes and onions, rice, salad, and fried bananas. There was a jar of worm-like peppers in vinegar - very hot and delicious. Fabi's food was fabulous!

After lunch, we went for a lagoon visit. As we sped ahead of our flotel, we had our first sightings of the plentiful pink river dolphins. Abruptly, we veered off into a small channel that was quickly clogged with aquatic plants. We plowed through, but Bambino had to reverse the outboard often to rid it of vegetation. Alvaro directed him from his perch in the prow. We saw ducks, cormorants, herons, hawks, eagles and hundreds of tinier birds. Eventually, we broke through, crossed the lagoon, and climbed out onto mud flats. In the wet season, we would be under water.

Iridescent beetles scurried from cracks in the mud. Beyond were shorter and taller grasses, where the snakes and caimans lived. Behind were trees, above water level, even in the rainy season. Nearby, a pink spoonbill began its strange feeding motion. A tall white and gray heron watched.

When we returned, we could barely detect where we had passed just before. A great excursion! Then, a few more hours of cruising, passing small riverside *chacras* (farms), passing dug-outs and small boats, with frequent dolphin sightings, and the ever-present sounds of the Amazon - birds, animals and insects. Awesome!

Dinner was fish, chicken, a fabulous cauliflower soufflé, potatoes, rice, juice and wine. After dinner, Christine departed at a village; a taxi waited. A short distance further, we tied up to the shore for the night.

When the generator was turned off at 21:00, on this overcast night, it was as though we were blind. There was absolutely no light from anywhere. We had no flashlight. We had to carefully navigate by feel our necessary bathroom trips.

Morning brought sun. We heard Ariel sweeping cobwebs that busy spiders had spun overnight. The jungle was awakening. Time for breakfast.

We ate banana, papaya, pineapple, bread, scrambled eggs, and ham. Coffee was a thick syrup you poured into your cup and added warm milk or hot water, and sugar, if desired.

By 9:00, we were again cruising the peaceful Ibare, now 50 to 100 meters wide, and totally jungle-lined. We passed *chacras* where bananas, yucca and sugar cane grew. Birds were everywhere. Pink dolphins were impossible to photograph. Monkeys climbed in the trees.

Frequently, Alvaro scouted ahead for larger approaching traffic. Maneuverability was limited and electronic communication non-existent. Sometimes we sat in the wheelhouse watching Bambino guide our slow passage. Mostly, we were on deck. It was so peaceful. There were no mosquitoes. River traffic passed. We were sure we could do this for a very long time.

At lunch, Gundy persuaded Fabi to join us and Alvaro. She shyly did. Fabi was single and had been the boat cook for five years. Lunch was chicken in a sauce, fish with limes, fried bananas, a beet, carrot, potato salad, noodles, and those wicked wormy chilies. Pink dolphins playfully broke the brown waters as we dined on this feast.

After lunch, a hammock siesta before the boat anchored at the confluence of the Ibare and larger Mamoré river. After siesta, we went up the Mamoré to fish for *piraña* amongst flooded trees. Again, Alvaro guided, and Bambino drove. Ariel cut beef for bait for our simple poles. Soon we were fishing. Gundy caught the first *piraña*, a beautiful gold color; she also caught the biggest, a red one. Bambino, Ariel and I also caught *pirañas*. Bigger *pirañas* bite hard, but smaller one's nibble. When we had enough for dinner, we went swimming in the same water as the *pirañas*!

Back on the *Reina*, we gave the *pirañas* to Fabi. Alvaro went swimming before washing some clothes in the river. Bambino and Ariel amused themselves unsuccessfully trying to fish with bow and arrow. Before dinner we enjoyed the sunset as the sky across the broad waters of the rivers, turned from gold to pink to red, framed in tropical fronds, images shimmering on dark waters.

The *pirañas* were served whole including tails, heads and sharp teeth, with cheesy rice, yucca, beef in mustard sauce, salad, fried eggplant, and wine.

On this clear night, there were stars - so many without the interference of lights! Bed comes early without electricity, but this night we had a flashlight.

And, we still had two more days in this special paradise.

Reina de Enín

To Marry a Mockingbird?
by Valerie Fletcher Adolph

I jumped from the dinghy into the warm water of the Pacific and waded up to the beach. The sun shone down on the white sand of the Island. This was Day Four of my retirement gift to myself – a trip to the Galapagos Islands. For a week I lived aboard a ship visiting most of the larger islands. The naturalists in the group came up the beach loaded with binoculars and cameras. Myself, I carried a small pocket camera; I wouldn't call myself a naturalist.

This morning our captain had announced that our ship needed to be re-fueled. Passengers were not allowed on board during re-fueling, so he would leave us to explore a nearby island for a few hours.

Great! Abandoned on a desert island! Another item off my bucket list. Why hadn't I paid more attention when I read Robinson Crusoe? My delight in the abstract idea of being abandoned on a desert island faded somewhat as I watched our ship heading out towards the horizon. In the light of reality, it became a more frightening concept. The boat would be coming back, wouldn't it?

The naturalist who came ashore with us allowed no time for worrying. While the sea lions were still huffing off, offended at our intrusion, he showed us the sat. phone, a first aid kit, water and snacks. He pointed to a steep hill some distance away and said several species of rare birds, including this island's rather rare mockingbird, could be seen near the top of this hill if anyone cared to make the hike. All the naturalists nodded eagerly. Only a couple of us elected to stay behind to relax on the beach. We promised to stay out of the sun and not to leave the area.

Off the birders went with their binoculars and cameras and most of the snacks. Linda, the other woman staying behind, and I agreed on the benefits of solitude. She set off to the south where sea lions were abundant. I turned north to where some thick bushes promised shelter from the sun. My plan was to catch up on my neglected trip diary.

I made myself a comfortable hollow in the sand resting my back on thick stems of the bushes and began to write. It was going well – I was remembering details, my pen traveling rapidly across the page until I heard a rustling in the leaves above me and became aware of a brown bird with a slightly curved beak regarding me with an accusing eye.

A mockingbird. Why wasn't it high on the hilltop to greet the real naturalists? I wondered if his nest was down here. Perhaps I was an intruder in these bushes. I looked around and couldn't see a nest. Maybe they just hollowed out the sand for a nest, much like I had done. Could I be sitting on it? I rolled to one side to look. No, no nest, no flattened egg shells. Still the accusing eye.

I studied the bird, wondering if indeed this was what everyone had hiked off to see. He still stared steadily at me. Somewhat disconcerted I politely told him that I knew this was his territory and added something trite about coming in peace.

To my surprise the accusing look disappeared, and he hopped down to a closer branch. He might not understand English but perhaps he liked the sound of my voice. Maybe no-one had ever spoken to him before.

So quietly, gently I explained the re-fueling, the group, my holiday, my diary. Head on one side he looked at me as if assessing the veracity of my story. Finished explaining, I went back to writing. Again a rustle and he was within a couple of feet of me watching my pen travel across the page. After several minutes he flew off. I supposed that the fascination of watching a moving pen had its limits.

Five minutes later he was back with a tiny shell in his beak, possibly a snail. He dropped it beside me. I picked it up and examined it, wondering what I was supposed to do with it. He spent a few moments looking at me, looking at the shell. Something was expected of me, but what?

He flew off again and was gone so long that I thought he must have given up on this strange visitor who did not know what to do with a perfectly good snail.

Ten minutes later he returned with something green twitching in his beak. He stared at me for a moment, head on one side. Then he dropped down to the sand beside me and with theatrical flourishes regurgitated one, two, three partially-digested but still moving green bugs. Hopping back on his branch he began preening his wing feathers.

I may not be a naturalist, but I recognize mating behavior when I see it. Interesting to observe, but un-nerving when I was expected to reciprocate. How does one respond to an amorous mockingbird? What was I supposed to do with half-digested green bugs? Bugs that might be the equivalent of champagne and caviar?

Thanking him politely, even profusely, I turned back to my writing, watching him out of the corner of my eye. He began collecting sticks, dropping them haphazardly beside the green bugs. Every now and then he looked up at me meaningfully.

I began to contemplate having a mockingbird as a mate. Lovely climate, beautiful beach, but the diet? Yuck! I went back yet again to my writing, disregarding the growing litter of sticks and the green bugs that now lay still.

Eventually my suitor grew tired of this perverse female and disappeared. I reflected on how lucky I'd been, not just to squint at a bird on a branch through binoculars but to interact with it for almost an hour.

Later the naturalists returned, hot and tired. "We didn't see the mockingbird," they said.

Padrón
by Ronald Mackay

"What does a Scotsman wear beneath his kilt?" - the quest of the curious since the first Scot belted himself into his woollen plaid.

In 1959, a bare 20 years after the Spanish Civil War ended, I made the first of my be-kilted forays into Franco's Spain. At the first sight of me, some primordial urge in the Latin psyche fired the entire population's curiosity and their drive to find out.

Attention had its up-side. The few drivers there were at that time would draw their cars or their lorries to an urgent halt. Sometimes they would go out of their way to take me to my destination. I've enjoyed lifts on carts drawn by mules and oxen. Horses and donkeys have borne my rucksack strapped to their backs affording their masters, under the pretext of lightening my burden, closer inspection of a rarity. On the downside, the noisy pursuit of ragged urchins or unashamedly curious adults, could become unbearable.

One night, I arrived at a village the outskirts of Santiago de Compostela, much too late to reach the town itself. The only inn was dark and locked down for the night.

"We're closed," came the answer when I rapped on the door. When I beat more urgently, a window flew open and a face appeared, but its anger was immediately replaced by consternation.

I took advantage of her wordlessness, "It is late. I am sorry. I need a room. Please!"

Wide-eyed, she observed me a moment longer and then I heard her voice inside. "Girls! Girls! Open the door, we have a guest. A man wearing a skirt!"

The innkeeper – for that's who the face belonged to -- and her two helpers couldn't do enough for me. They showed me to a spotless room. When I mentioned that I hadn't eaten since breakfast, they heated a tureen of soup and refilled my bowl until I'd supped the last drop.

The next morning all three served me breakfast. I did my best to answer their questions. 'Who was I?' 'Where did I come from?' 'Did my mother know I was away from home alone?' 'Where was I going?' 'Did I speak a Christian language?' All the while their admiring eyes were on my kilt. 'Was it made of wool?' 'Why were the pleats so deep?' 'What was the leather purse for?'

Fortunately, they refrained from asking more intimate questions, though by their looks and gestures, these questions were on their mind.

On telling the three that I had no plans for the day, they recommended I take the train to the hamlet of Padrón.

"Today Padrón celebrates its annual fair. The local farmers show their best milk-cows, their finest goats -- and the roosters! You will see none prouder! They will trade horses. And the octopus – it is delicious!"

The hamlet of Padrón was at least two kilometres distant from its railway station.

I left the crowded train with what seemed hundreds of passengers trailing enthusiastically behind me, pointing at and commenting on the rhythmic swing of my kilt.

At a crossroads crowded with vehicles that included those drawn by ox, ass and draught-horse all heading for the fair, two astonished Civil Guards stopped the traffic in all directions to let me and my admirers pass. Just as I was about to cross, a woman raced up and whispered something in the officers' ears.

"You! Man-in-the-skirt!" they cried together, pointing. "Stop!"

I had learned to obey armed Civil Guards without question. I had no wish to test the marksmanship of the one with the rifle nor of his partner with the machine gun. I stopped, and right there in the middle of the crossroads with impatient traffic waiting, they peppered me with the usual questions.

"Where are you from?" "Does your mother know you are away from home alone?" "Do you speak a Christian language?" "Where are you going?" All the while admiring my kilt. Even the drivers descended from their carts, ancient cars and dilapidated lorries to join the wondering throng.

Suddenly, a brilliant idea seemed to strike the drab Civil Guards. Or perhaps it was quietly suggested to them by the enterprising young woman on whose initiative they had originally accosted me.

"It's too far for you to walk to the fairgrounds!" Said the first Guard. The young woman nodded her approval.

Were they banning me from the fair? I was already almost there. Scores were heading in the same direction, on foot like me. I could see and hear the flare and blare of the fairground through the trees in the distance.

"Too far? No comprendo!" I was confused and becoming aggrieved. Civil Guard or no Civil Guard, I hadn't paid for the train ticket to Padrón and walked more than half way from the station just to be peremptorily turned away the very moment before I'd reached my destination.

"Much too far!" Agreed the second Civil Guard. Again, the entrepreneurial young woman was nodding emphatically, encouraging what I took to be their pestering of me.

"We'll find you a lift to the fairground!"

A lift? So, their aim was facilitation not obstruction! I looked at them with fresh eyes.

And a lift I got. Refusal was out of the question. A great, levitating hoist up onto the back of a creaky lorry laden with bales of fragrant hay for the fairground.

Both Civil Guards, the enthusiastic young woman and scores of merry-makers old and young who refused to be left out of the fun and the revealing public display, joyfully upraised me until I sat atop the itchy bales.

That is why, today, of all the folks in any region of Spain, those of Padrón will confidently tell you from knowledge gained first-hand, what a Scotsman wears under his kilt.

Bear Necessities
by Alyson Hilbourne

We ignored the sign in the tourist office which urged us to rent bear bells. Frankly we've seen little wildlife in Japan: a *tanuki* (raccoon dog) scavenging in a plastic bag in the street at a ski resort, and snow monkeys at the hot water springs, but in all the miles we've hiked we've never seen anything other than birds.

We were preparing to walk part of the Nakasendo, an old road that ran between Tokyo and Kyoto during the Edo period. The post towns of Tsumago and Magome have many preserved wood and plaster buildings that show how the towns would have looked some two or three hundred years ago, and the seven-kilometre hike between them is along a well-signposted trail.

Our route from Tsumago took us up the river valley. The morning mist was burning off to reveal early cherry trees flowering on the water's edge. The path was mostly gravelly, well maintained and easy to follow. As we disappeared into the forest, redwoods towered over us and bamboo groves rattled in the wind. We criss-crossed the river on wooden bridges and passed through tiny hamlets, which were probably way stations in the past, with overnight accommodation for travellers. We stopped at a waterfall for photographs and a chocolate break. We ignored several brass bells on poles, thinking they were temple bells of some sort, until we came across one with a notice attached.

"Ring the bell hard against bears."

We dutifully rang.

Hard.

And we scanned the path ahead of us, carefully. Asian black bears might be smaller than their brown bear cousins, and might be mainly herbivores, but there is no knowing when they may decide chocolate should be part of their diet.

About halfway along the trail we were welcomed into the Tateba Tea House by an elderly gentleman wearing a conical woven bamboo hat and something akin to blue cotton pyjamas. Actually, it would have been difficult not to stop, as he practically blocked our path. He served us green tea and crunchy preserved plums. Since he had almost no English and we had little conversational Japanese there was a lot of smiling and bowing. Because we were getting along so well, he broke into some opera and serenaded us, not a word of which we understood. But there was no mention of bears.

The wooden tea house couldn't have changed in a hundred years. A traditional fireplace, *irori*, was set in the raised wooden floor, and a blackened kettle hung over the burning embers, while the room beyond had *tatami* mats for sleeping. When the old man's song was finished, we signed the visitors' book, glancing swiftly for any previous mention of bears and waved goodbye.

We continued over the pass, checking the path, and ringing a few more bells on our way. We met a man, a foreigner like us, walking the other way. He was constantly peering about and seemed very nervous.

"Have you seen any bears?" He asked after we'd said hello.

"No." We laughed. Nervously.

It was then, as we were coming down into the town of Magome, we noticed that the fields and gardens on the outskirts were enclosed with wire fences and topped off with electric cables.

"Maybe there is a bear problem here," I said, as a vision flashed through my mind of a bear sitting in a paddy field, gently plucking the rice shoots.

Since we had elected to walk back rather than catch the bus, we rang all the bells we saw, and checked constantly along the path in front and behind. We returned to our guesthouse much relieved we'd seen nothing but the odd bird on the route and feeling perhaps we'd escaped lightly.

When we got back, we asked our host.

"Are there bears around here?"

"Oh, yes," he nodded. "But not on the hiking trail. People who go up into the mountains to collect mushrooms see them. The bells are to educate the bears and keep them off the Nakasendo. You didn't see any?" He looked at us.

I shook my head.

"So, the bells are working then."

"But what about the electric fences?" I asked. "Are they for the bears?"

"Wild pigs," he said. "The eat everything. They have wet noses, so they don't like electric."

Darn. I rather liked the idea of bears in the paddy fields. Still, I'm glad we didn't rent bells. The continuous noise would have spoiled the walk.

And the bears are obviously well educated anyway.

Bear Bell

Tackling the Tanami Track
by Robyn Boswell

The final decision came as we reached the turn-off north of Alice Springs. The signpost said it all – Halls Creek 1032kms. That was it; the next town. In between was the Tanami Desert. We'd debated for days as to whether we'd tackle the desert crossing and had listened to advice that mostly said "No, don't do it", but there we were, loaded with water, diesel and enough supplies in case of a breakdown.

We'd read as much as we could about how to be safe, so when Noel stopped and said "Well, should we?" we all chorused "Yes" and our destiny was set.

The first 125kms were twelve-foot wide bitumen, comfortable to drive on, but when a car came towards you it was a game of chicken to see who would lose their nerve first and pull off into the red dust on the side. Fortunately, we only saw three cars all morning and by day's end had seen all six cars that we would meet on the whole track.

We passed the signpost to Yuendumu, an aboriginal settlement that you needed a permit to visit and the last sign of civilization for 350 kms apart from a very few lonely signs that indicated there were isolated cattle stations at the end of driveways that were 125 kilometres or more long. What a hard life some people signed up to!

Leaving the seal behind we drove on red gravel as wide as a 6-lane highway. As the road became too corrugated, the grader simply graded new lanes on the sides of the existing road. Fortunately, we were on the track soon after the grader had paid a rare visit. We had to keep our speed up to skim across the top of the corrugations, but at the same time the spotter in the passenger seat had to keep their eyes peeled for bulldust, lighter than the rest of the road, which filled deep holes that would break an axle or the towbar of Little Blue, our trusty trailer, if we crashed into them. Bouncing and swerving along the road set up a cacophony of sound as everything in the landcruiser swayed and jolted.

We stopped for a picnic lunch right on the road; no need to pull over. Instantly we were aware that we were mere specks in the endless panorama of spinifex and red dust. The wind sang across the desert as it had done since the dawn of time. Humans were insignificant in this untouched wilderness. It was one of those rare moments in life when you feel your whole body zinging with the joy of being alive and being part of something greater than yourself.

The hours rolled by and the spinifex and dust went on and on. We played Trivial Pursuits to pass the time, until late in the afternoon we encountered a small, green building and a petrol pump that was almost lost in the grandeur of the landscape. This was our destination for the night, Rabbit Flat, the most remote roadhouse in Australia, 650 kms from Alice Springs and 454 kms from Halls Creek. We erected our tents in the campground out the back beside a billabong and lit a campfire to cook our steaks for dinner, marvelling at the fact that we were alone in the majesty of the Australian desert. Suddenly we heard the unmistakable growl of a diesel engine and a bus rolled into the camp, full of scouts from Melbourne on a grand adventure. So much for solitude!

The next morning, as we sat in the cool of a desert sunrise eating breakfast, a green and gold cloud of thousands upon thousands of budgerigars billowed over the billabong. We watched, fascinated, as they swooped and dipped, ensuring that every member of the flock got a sip of water as they passed by.

We chatted to the proprietor for a while. It turned out there were some mines not too far away and some aboriginal settlements deep in the desert. We'd wondered why he had a bar in the roadhouse. He showed us the loaded rifle he kept under the counter 'just in case things get out of hand'. He only had to pull it out and place it on the counter for things to calm down. He was about to go 'up the road a little way', 300 kilometres or so to the nearest airstrip to pick up his sons who were flying in from boarding school over 4000kms away in Melbourne.

Shortly into our second long day we passed into Western Australia. The road deteriorated markedly becoming very narrow, sandy, heavily corrugated and lined by yellow grasses almost as tall as the Landcruiser, which made it virtually impossible to spot oncoming traffic. Fortunately, we didn't meet any other vehicles all day. Termite mounds got taller and taller and we stopped by one that towered over our vehicle, the tiny, busy denizens hidden in its cool depths.

We overnighted at Carranya Station, an isolated cattle station with a very dusty campsite. My airbed went down so I spent the night in one of our deckchairs, mesmerised by the chandelier of stars strung across the heavens and the golden glow of sunrise in the Australian bush.

At Wolf Creek Meteorite Crater we climbed the walls, marvelled at the 800m wide perfect circle formed by an ancient meteorite and pondered on the impact such an event must have had on the entire planet.

As we traversed the last 100 or so kilometres of dust and corrugations we discovered Little Blue was worse for wear. The towbar had bent with the constant banging and crashing. We held on with a wing and a prayer until we found ourselves back on a smooth tarmac road with a few kilometres to go to Halls Creek.

The four of us cheered as we hit the bitumen. We'd not only made it, we'd had an incredible adventure that would stay with us forever. We'd conquered the Tanami Desert!

To Italy and back
by Andrew Klein

In 1985, while traveling with my friend Geno, we chanced upon a small, but lovely, place along the French Riviera, called Menton. This was the last French villa on the coast and just two stops from Italy on the train line. Geno's family had immigrated from Italy, and he was somewhat anxious to set foot into the 'old country'. Just a few miles east of Menton, across the border, sat the small city of Ventimiglia. We did not think to stop at this coastal town, as we would be going on to Genoa, but its significance to our trip remains somewhat of a sore spot.

Geno and I had been friends for twelve years, and we were completely aware of the idea that one of us might need some 'private' time in life. I mean, after all, we grew up together. We shared a dorm room at San Diego State, and later a beach house nearby. We were comfortable with each other and respected each other's needs. We had recently met two young Norwegian girls who were traveling around Europe together, and quickly became friends. We had meals with them, went to the beach together, and shared evening drinks as well. On one such evening, we were out on the town, it was quite lovely, and, I must admit, somewhat romantic. Geno's 'date' became a bit amorous, and the two of them decided that while the night certainly wasn't over, it was time to return to our hotel. He whispered in my ear, 'Give me a few hours before coming back'. My girl and I were not so attracted by pheromones, but we were still quite friendly and enjoyed each other's company. We smiled at the others as they walked off in the direction of the hotel Parisian. Now, what were we going to do for the next 3 hours? As previously mentioned, Helena and I were not lovers, but we were not cold either. I took her hand and we walked to a shop where we purchased a couple of Kronenborgs. We talked about our travel plans. We were leaving the next day, and they were on to visit France. As we walked on, we crossed the street to the beach side. Menton is sometimes called the prettiest town in France, and there are several reasons for this. One is its gardens, which we had already visited, another is its string of romantic eateries along the coast, which we had only just enjoyed, and another is its proximity to the beautiful Mediterranean Sea, which we were about to get intimate with.

For days, we had enjoyed the sun and sands of this part of the Riviera. The weather had been wonderful, and the sights, well, I'm sure the reader can picture what lovely sights were availed to the wandering eyes, as we lay on that beach. The water was so blue, and its temperature very inviting. We took daily swims as did most every visitor. However, on this fine evening, we decided to walk on the same beach which was crowded with tourists in the day but, had not a one at that moment. We held each other and took in the beauty of the occasion.

There was a guy who rented beach items in the day. One thing he rented was paddle boats, and while most of his inventory was safely locked away in his cabana, these were too large to put up. Helena and I had already indulged in a few libations and we were feeling rather sprightly. We devised a plan to 'borrow' one of the boats, go out to sea a bit, turn around, finish our beers, and return it as briskly as possible. We pulled the heavy craft to the shoreline, took off our shoes, and pushed it into the water. We jumped in and after some difficulty, figured out how to steer it and off we went. After about ten minutes we were out far enough, and we turned to see a most charming sight. The lights of Menton were stunning. If we would have been lovers, I'm not sure this would be the end of this story. It was beautiful, and we both commented on its loveliness, and how romantic it was. The stars, the moon, the scene was from a film. I noticed another similar sight but a few kilometers down the coast. Helena said, 'that's Ventimiglia, Italy'. That was all I needed. If Geno was going to keep me from getting a good night's rest, I was going to go to Italy before him.

We agreed to go and began a 45-minute paddle to the shores of Italia. We were excited. We hit land, jumped out, and pulled the craft up the beach. We went across the street and into a local pub. We ordered Italian beers and marveled at the difference in taste from the French ones. We talked with some folks and before long it was late. Like a couple of 'Cinderellas' we ran out, crossed the street, hopped into our 'carriage' and paddled back to France arriving just short of 3am. We carefully replaced the boat and laughed our way to the hotel. The old Lady cursed us as she let us in, and I walked Helena to her room and said goodnight. We would all take breakfast together in the morning.

When I got back Geno was alone. He rolled over and asked, 'where were you?' I simply said, 'I left the country, but I came back for you!'. He figured it out and expressed his agitation. I told him to go to sleep. He realized it was his fault, and stopped yipping, but the rest of the trip I think he held it against me that I had gone to Italy without him. I fell asleep that night, thinking of Norwegian company, stars, lights and water, and in the morning woke up wondering why my legs hurt so!

Himalaya – Retellings
by Sourabha Rao

Recollections from travel journal entries made in Ladakh, Kashmir. September 2016.

Himaalaya, my dear, dear sweet calamity.

Self-conscious. I belong to a species that is self-conscious. Knowledge rests in us. Seeking drives us.

Today, I stand here before you, surrounded by you, leaving myself to the mystery and mercy of your enormous being. I am in Khardung La, the world's highest motorable pass. As far as my vision reaches out to, I see your mountains immersing in and emerging out from more mountains... a spectacular, gigantic labyrinth. I see snow sparkling softly, silently in the morning sun.

In the past one week, apart from the mountain-dwellers and travellers, I have also seen many little animals living in the lap of you. The Himalayan pika has been a favourite little creature. In a valley in North Pullu, I befriended a handsome, furry dog briefly while a few yaks were grazing around. It was hard to leave him as he had taken me deep into the valley and we sat by a stream and heard its sweet gurgle. I drank from the clear stream before bidding the dog a goodbye and the sweetness of the cold water still lingers on my tongue. What an infinite network of symbiotic existences. A whole – a symbiotic, organic, inseparable whole.

Dear Himaalaya,

These are foggy unbecomings... similar to how one feels in love, at least in the beginning of it. I have fallen in love with your mighty silence, even your ruthless silence, your now-and-forever silence. How could one ever tell the difference between foolishness and innocence in such love? As for me, I would settle for anything.

Beholding you in my greedy vision was a dream and today, in your presence, I simply feel like the shadow of my own dream. It isn't like you have embraced me with love and warmth... in fact, I thought I would freeze to death when I stayed in a tent by Tso Moriri (Lake Moriri) a couple of days ago. Last week was tough living in these great heights. The night sky was glorious as the spine of the Milky Way could be seen with naked eye, but the bitter cold was as brutal as it could have been. However, such suffering is better than the onslaughts of circumstances that occur in my usual world, to which I have to fly back tomorrow.

Before I came to you, there was an incisive curiosity about you in my mind. I was lured by the illusion of finding 'answers' to questions that weren't even formed fully. But here, I have existed in a way where everything felt unbearably real and trance-like at the same time... I belong to a species that is self-conscious. Knowledge rests in us. Seeking drives us. But you have liberated me from intellectual fatigue. I have existed beyond an intellect to explore, learn... beyond even a mind to emote... With you, I have belonged, I have felt home.

Tomorrow, I will soar high to reach tremendous heights beyond clouds. A plane, a marvel made possible by some of the greatest minds of my species, will take me up above your peaks. The same species that's also capable of war and destruction like no other. This trance might not remain in its purest form as I get back to where I came from, but something has already changed.

When I go back and tell your story, my story, our story, I will always try to limn a tender world in my writing because it's still a possibility – a world so gentle that it's devoid of war and differences. As I fly high, from where the worldly details lose their meaning beautifully, carrying memories of you and all their suggestiveness putting everything into perspective, I will pray for a world with no borders that lead to violence, a world merging into a single, unbroken expanse of beauty. A prayer in those heights, even as I pale into insignificance.

Khardung La

The Temples of Angkor in Cambodia
by Tom Czaban

It was just a short ride from the centre of Siem Reap, but vendors assaulted the bus windows the entire way. They rapped their dirty knuckles on the wet glass to sell fruit, baguettes and foreign newspapers. But I wasn't there for food or newspapers; I had come to see the Eighth Wonder of the World.

On the bus, there was a simultaneous gasp when Angkor Wat's magnificent turrets appeared. I'd seen many temples in the previous weeks, but Angkor was special. Its ruins rose out of the dust like a scene from an *Indiana Jones* movie.

I followed the umbrellas off the bus and toward the complex; it grew in size and magnificence with each soggy step. Johann Wolfgang von Goethe, a German poet and author, once wrote: "Architecture is frozen music."

And, at Angkor, it really is.

Etched into the crumbling walls were pictures from everyday Khmer life. I had seen these scenes before: Not in books or history programs, but in the Cambodian villages I had just left behind. People danced beneath the sun; men fished in rivers; and girls rested in their mother's laps after a long day.

All around me, tourists in anoraks pondered the ruins. Their luminous umbrellas made it even more beautiful — enlivening the grey buildings with dazzling colour. The rain drove down upon us, the smell of hot soil filled the air, everyone was soaked but didn't seem to mind.

Amongst the tourists, I noticed an old English couple. English people try hard not to say the wrong thing, but often end up doing exactly that. On this occasion, the friendly English woman patted her Cambodian guide and gestured to a scene on the wall.

"Wow monkeys!" she exclaimed.

Her guide looked at her with confusion; her face fell as she studied the etchings again.

"Oh dear. I do apologise. They're not monkeys; they're people." She added, "I beg your pardon," then shuffled off in embarrassment.

A few hours later, the rain stopped but the umbrellas remained open to deflect the sun. Astonishingly, tourists were permitted to clamber over the ruins. In Europe, everything is roped off — with signs warning visitors to keep out. But here, the only signs warned tourists to take care of themselves.

"Do not walk this way. Sorry if this is an inconvenience."

For some reason it seemed sarcastic; it wasn't what the sign said, but more the way it said it.

At the top of Bayon temple, I passed an elderly American. His bones looked as brittle as the stones beneath his feet, but he skipped along them with the energy of a child.

"This is worth a million dollars!" he shouted, pulling his camera from his pocket. "My God! Look how they built the roof!"

His wife just nodded.

"You will help me get down, won't you?" she fretted. "I'm OK getting up; it's the getting down I don't like."

"Yeah of course," he shot back, still looking through his viewfinder.

I sat down on a wall and watched a group of monks walk the top tier. One of them was taking photos as if his life (lives?) depended on it. They ignored the other tourists and made a beeline for me. For some reason, monks like me. Perhaps it's my shaved head?

"Hello?" said the monk with the camera, "Can I speak with you to practice my English?"

"Sure," I replied, already wishing I'd declined because a crowd had gathered to watch.

"Please excuse me," the monk continued. "My English is very bad, so don't mind if it is impolite or incorrect."

"It's fine," I replied.

"Thank you for your understanding. Now, can I ask? What is your name?"

"Tom."

"Good. And Tom, how many people are there in your family?"

Embarrassed, I began to tell him about myself. Most of the spectators had cameras in their hands and desperately tried to find a shot without me in it.

The monks were visiting from Southern Cambodia and were excited as they never had been here before. We all agreed the temples were amazing — and that speaking English is hard.

Then they asked to take a photo with me. Reluctantly, I agreed.

"Ok," barked the monk. "You come here! Now! Get up!"

He was very bossy, especially for a monk.

"Alright, I'm coming," I said.

"Quickly!" he urged. "Hurry up!"

I couldn't understand the rush. I thought we were all going to get reborn anyway?

When he'd finished directing the photo shoot, I left them to it. There was a collective sigh of relief from the other tourists, swiftly followed by a flurry of camera flashes.

Soon it was time to return to the bus, which once again was surrounded by vendors. One of them wouldn't leave me alone; she followed me right up to the bus door.

"I have book, with map," she said.

"I don't need it, thank you."

"Do you want cold drink? I have Coke."

"No thank you. I don't need it."

"Do you want hot drink? I have tea."

"No thank you. I don't need it."

"So, tell me, what do you need?"

"Nothing," I told her.

I assumed that would be the end of it. I was wrong.

"Ok," she said. "I will sell you nothing, for two dollars."

I couldn't help but smile.

This must have been how the Khmers conceived and built this staggering complex — intelligence and persistence.

That was what I was thinking... as I bought the overpriced Coke.

The coldest winter, the warmest hearts
by Wenlin Tan

Two disorientating nights in Tokyo – squished like sanma in a tin can with the rush hour crowd commuting along the Yamanote line; stunned like a deer in headlights at the billboards in dizzying colours and fonts all around the Shibuya crossing; confused like a chameleon in a bag of skittles by the spiderweb of metro lines – are enough to convince me: *Tokyo is not for me.* Thankfully, two nights is all I have, and with a sigh of relief, I flee on the bullet train to the north-east.

Three hours later, the serenity of Ishinomaki is a welcome escape- save for a few people at the bus station, the square is completely empty; aside from the gusts of wind streaming in, there is barely a sound. The hair of my skin immediately stands at attention to the frigid air around me, a gentle reminder of how ill-equipped I am for the cold. A borrowed woollen coat the shade of wisteria in full bloom, something (if given a choice) I would never be caught dead in, becomes my most prized possession, shielding me for the next few days.

Affectionately dubbed 'rock and roll city', a literal translation of 'Ishinomaki' 石巻, the rural town lies in Miyagi Prefecture, nestled along the Sanriku coast. Most Japanese know it as the area that was hit hardest by the 2011 Tsunami and Tohoku earthquake. My trip here is a happy accident- an acquaintance introduced me to an educational tourism project, Boundless, which runs tours in rural areas. Wanting to venture somewhere off the beaten track, I jumped at the chance to visit.

During an orientation of the city, I am introduced to the concept/term 'Inaka' (田舎) by Dennis, a lanky Singaporean who's the mastermind behind Boundless.

'Inaka translates to 'rural area' or 'countryside, but there is also the misconception that people here are unsophisticated or backward', Dennis shrugs apologetically.

I nod empathetically, not giving much thought.

The initiatives I am introduced to – wake up calls from fisherman to rebrand their image in people's minds by Yahoo and Fisherman Japan, opportunities for small restaurateurs to build their businesses by renting food trucks at a low rent at Hashidori Common, and free IT classes on software development by local start-up ITNAV – convince me that Ishinomaki is anything *but* backward.

An encounter during on the coldest night during my five days there, however, is what leaves a lasting impression.

Late in the evening after dusk, we alight the bus at a stop along a dimly-lit road. We shuffle in the freezing cold, my fingers numb, buried deep in my coat pockets, and my nose hidden beneath my scarf. There is a slight rancidity in the air, a byproduct of the seafood processing factories we pass along our way. I struggle to pay attention to the road, following behind Dennis blindly.

Reaching a grey-roofed warehouse, Dennis knocks on the door gently. After a brief pause, the door creaks open, and we are welcomed into the headquarters of Ishinomaki lab.

Chief marketer David, a genial bespectacled Canadian, shows us around the two-storey workspace with cream coloured walls and crimson red railings.

On the first floor, hand tools and power tools are strewn over long wooden workbenches where three craftsmen are hard at work. Huge logs of wood are stacked to the far end of the facility, and a rustic-looking heater is just behind us. I beeline for the heater, sighing in relief as my fingers thaw like frozen sausages over a campfire.

We are introduced to Chiba san, a well-built middle-aged man with smiling eyes, the creator of Ishinomaki lab. A former sushi chef and local, he noticed that following the onslaught of the tsunami, there were hardly any common spaces for residents to come together.

'Let's make some simple furniture, put it in public areas and see what happens,' he thought. This is how Ishinomaki lab was born.

As we survey their creations, my gaze lands on an AA stool, their earliest and most famous design. The peculiar shape of a logo, etched on the side of the stool, catches my eye. The words, 'Ishinomaki lab' are contained within a box-like square, with a small opening on the top right corner.

'Do you know why it's is designed this way?' David asks.

After pondering a moment, I shake my head.

'We intentionally left this space, to remind us to be open to new ideas and welcome perspectives from outside, always.'

At this, something stirs in me- a feeling I can't quite put my finger on. But time is up, and we have a go at heat embossing on a small wooden block, a souvenir for our visit, before leaving. Subsequently, those words and that memory settle into the background, like how most memories do. But the thing that stirred within me never settled- in fact, it resurfaced, getting stronger each time.

The days fly by, and before I realise, I am on the bus waiting in Ishinomaki, looking out the window at the town square, recalling the moment I arrived, freezing from the curt politeness and alienation of Tokyo.

Memories from the past few days flood my mind: smiles and hugs from residents, locals and non-locals alike; colourful individuals, including a Kagoshima native who hunts deer, fishes and makes wooden houses from scratch, a British man who is the director of the local community centre, a Kanazawa native who works at the town hall – many of whom came to Ishinomaki to help with the reconstruction efforts and never left; the logo, those words from Ishinomaki lab; and the term, 'Inaka'.

And I realise: the warmth of Inaka, this was what was stirring inside.

The bus captain gets on the bus into his seat, announcing that the time is approximately 22:10 and will departing for Tokyo. I smile, and wave a silent goodbye to the station, knowing this won't be the last time I visit.

Because the secret of Ishinomaki is, *the warmth of Inaka welcomes you anytime.*

What happened to the corn on the cob?
by Lindsay de Feliz

When I had been living in the Dominican Republic for around six months, I started going out with a Dominican man, called Danilo, who eventually became my husband. He decided he wanted to show me where he had been raised, 3,000 feet up in the mountains above the city of Barahona.

Barahona, the name of the province and its capital city, is in the south west of the Dominican Republic, around 114 miles west of the capital, Santo Domingo. The province covers 347 square miles and Barahona city is only 93 miles from the Haitian border. The drive from Barahona along the coast to the border is said to be the most beautiful drive in the Caribbean.

What makes Barahona so special is its wild and natural landscape. There are towering mountains which literally descend into the Caribbean Sea, rivers running down from the mountains, flowing alongside the beaches and into the sea, tropical rain forests, unspoiled and deserted beaches of smooth colourful pebbles or white powdery sand. Given the lack of development, lack of tourism and the stunning natural beauty, it is home to a variety of wildlife including crocodiles, iguanas, and flamingos and is a bird lovers' paradise.

We rented an SUV, known as a *jipeta* and off we set on a long drive, over four hours, all along the southern coast of the country going west, and my first time driving in the Dominican Republic as Danilo couldn't drive. We drove through the capital where the driving is the craziest I have ever seen, especially with Danilo navigating yelling, "Turn left" when I was in the right-hand lane and screaming, "Go" even though the traffic lights were on red.

We drove through the towns of San Cristobal and Bani, and eventually the landscape changed into desert, with cacti sticking up everywhere then slowly the mountains came into view, rising majestically above the blue Caribbean ocean and on the right at the foot of the mountains were sugar cane fields as far as the eye could see. As we moved closer, I could see Haitian men, stripped to the waist with the sweat glistening on their muscular bodies as they chopped the cane, the same way as it had been done for centuries. The hump-backed oxen stood in the shade of the trees swatting the myriads of flies from their backs with their raggedy tails waiting patiently to haul the cane in wooden carts onto the waiting train. It was like another world.

The next day we drove along the coast road, stopping at Los Patos, where one of the shortest rivers in the world at 61 metres runs down from the mountains and flows into the ocean. We bathed in cold river water, whilst looking at the sea and feasting on fresh fish and drinking frosty *Presidente* beer.

We drove high up into the mountains, so I could see where Danilo had been brought up and meet some old friends of his father who were making charcoal, just as his dad used to as it was the main fuel supply for cooking. Trees would be cut down and the green wood piled into a pyramid. A hole would be left in the middle, into which a very dry piece of wood would be inserted. The pyramid would be covered with soil and the dry stick in the middle lit. The pile of wood would burn slowly for up to five days until the end result was a large pile of charcoal.

One of his father's friends was called *El Viejo*, which means old man and he was in his 80s. He invited us into his little house and asked if I would like some coffee. I accepted readily, expecting he would go and put the kettle on. But there was no kettle and there was no electricity. He went out into the garden and picked some coffee beans. He then lit the charcoal on the outside cooking stove called a *fogon* which is basically a cement table. He then roasted the fresh beans in a pan, together with some sugar, and once roasted he crushed them in a *pilon*, or pestle and mortar. Then he put them into a sort of muslin bag on a stick and poured boiling water through them and added more sugar. Although it took well over an hour to make, it was the most amazing coffee I have ever tasted in my life.

I wanted to go to the toilet and whispered to Danilo to ask where it was. He pointed in the direction of a little hut at the bottom of the garden. I walked gingerly towards it, picking my way over the rocks, avoiding the chickens and the two small pigs, and cautiously pulled open the rotting wooden door. There was an upturned crate with a hole in it and I hovered uncomfortably above it, grateful I always had a wad of toilet paper in my pocket. At the side of this tiny hut, on the ground, was a pile of corn on the cob, but no corn just the husks.

When I left the latrine, I questioned Danilo about them. "Do people eat corn when they're sitting on the toilet? Is it some Dominican tradition I haven't heard of?" He looked at me blankly. "What you say?"

"Well, there is a pile of empty husks in the toilet," I explained.

He still looked blank and as realisation dawned, he howled with laughter, "Those are *tusas*. You use to wipe bottom. Is very good toilet paper."

Apparently, the corncobs are given to the chickens which eat the corn, and the empty cobs are stacked in the latrine to be used as required. I didn't try one.

El Viejo's House

Bucket List: Number 1 – Slieve League
by Mike Cavanagh

I'd never really thought about having a 'Bucket List' before I started planning on a trip to the UK and Ireland in 1993. My partner, Katie, and I managed to wrangle over six months off work and were planning on a mini-European adventure, mainly though focussing on the UK and Ireland. While it was Katie who originally mooted the idea, as she'd been OS a number of times while I hadn't (apart from New Zealand, which really doesn't count when you're an Ozzie!), I quickly gained enthusiasm as we researched where we'd like to go. We had a notebook we used to list all the places we thought sounded good to stay, mainly BnBs and self-catering cottages, but my main job was to collect info on 'where' we wanted to go: castles, mansions, gardens, national parks, walks, drives, all that sort of stuff.

Two small booklets we got from the local tourist centre set me off on my 'bucket list', and I determined that above all else I wanted to walk the Slieve League sea cliffs in Donegal, Ireland, visit The Skelligs off the south west coast of Ireland, and get to St Kilda, a rocky, windswept island 70kms west of the Scottish mainland. As tends to be my wont, having set my mind to these things, 'obsession' is probably a fair and accurate assessment of my determination, hence my bucket list began with these three places. Each place seemed to echo in me my desire for the wild – winds, wild seas, craggy, beetling cliffs, and cloud torn skies; places isolated from the heavy hand of civilisation where nature in its primal rawness can be experienced. Yes, well, I do tend to the romantic as well, so it seems.

So, did I manage to tick them all off? Well, no. St Kilda remained out of reach, and still does these 25 years on. Slieve League and The Skelligs... hmmm, no, yes, sort of, but not as I had hoped.

The day we parked to walk Slieve League began promisingly; sunny, mild, blue skies, light breeze. My hopes were high as we set off to traipse up to the top of these 2,000-foot-high cliffs, the highest sea cliffs in Europe so I'd been informed by the little tourist book. Ah, but this was Ireland after all and 'soft weather' is always just around the corner. We'd learned that soft weather could mean anything from a short-lived pea soup fog to constant drizzle for days that left any patch of ground a quagmire.

Half way up we stopped to admire the view. Three hundred metres below us already, down the vertiginous, twisted rocks of these towering cliffs, the broad, sun-kissed, blue-green swathe of the Atlantic swept away to the horizon with nothing but ocean between us and the 'next stop', Labrador, Canada. The cloudless sky seemed to roll along above us, a fresh-washed, blue canopy over what portended as one of those perfect days when you feel you can reach out and touch the hand of God, or as Jimi Hendrix put it: 'scuse me while I kiss the sky. A dense bank of low cloud sliding around the point of Slieve League was the only issue for concern, but with only half an hours walk to go, of no concern, surely?

Twenty minutes later we were stumbling along, cold, dripping wet, cocooned within a saturating, dense blanket of cloud with visibility down to about ten metres. We could only surmise we were still on the track as we hadn't fallen off the cliffs and the little rills of water forming tended to do so in the middle of the bare path. We pressed on, hoping the clouds would lift, part, vaporise, anything, so we could take in the view we were so doggedly now aspiring to.

At the top of Slieve League, the land falls away on both sides, and the path along the ridge is called 'One Man's Path' for very good reason. On a fine, fair day, no place for the faint hearted then. In this now wretched weather, slippery underfoot, with our cold wet bodies beginning to shiver (foolishly we'd been lured by the earlier sunshine and blue skies to venture forth from the car in light summer clothing), and no foreseeable views to come, literally, we stopped.

Sitting on the rocks, we stuffed ourselves with chocolate bars to warm ourselves and bemoaned the desperately disappointing turn in the weather. If anything, the cloud bank was darkening, the heavy mist turning to drizzle, the sort that says, 'I think I'll just hang around for forty days or so.' After twenty minutes, we gave up and headed back down to the car.

It was slowish going back down, the path now sheened in a thin cover of mud that threatened to send our feet flying at every step. Forty minutes later we were back at our car, out of the clouds, and drying and warming ourselves as best we could. We were booked to be in a cottage that afternoon quite some distance away, then further on after that, and on a ferry to Scotland the day after that. This had been my one chance, this trip, to tick Slieve League' off my list. Despondent, we drove off, away, promising 'next time'.

A quarter of a century later, and 'next time' still hasn't arrived. Disappointed? Yes, but...

Truth is, I wanted to see these wild places because they are wild, not picture postcards, pretty views to admire, tick off, before moving off to another; 'railway carriage charm' as so aptly said by Van Morrison, Ireland's living breathing songwriter/poet/ madman.

Well, hadn't I got what I came for, then? And what's more, I'd had my cake and eaten it too: been there and it's still on my list. Seriously, what was there to complain about?

So, fair play to you Slieve League; fair play to you.

As for The Skelligs... well, that's another story.

Walking Mdina to Valletta
by Lee P. Ruddin

'Hello again!' said Jonathan, a Costa barista so well built you'd think he'd been constructed at Cammell Laird shipyard.

This coffeeshop, within the Embassy Shopping Complex on St. Lucia Street in Valletta, isn't situated in the prettiest of surroundings: dated shop facia and bland floor tiles ensure it's a place only those nostalgic for the Soviet Union would add to their bucket lists.

I tried my utmost to avoid visiting a coffee chain, but the cup sizes in Caffe Cordina would only provide a caffeine fix for a Lilliputian. I entered Costa after the same Borrowers-like measures were served in cafés along Republic Street, though after deeming the coast clear — presumably much like a man does before entering a certain establishment.

Any thoughts of being labelled a philistine by those in the European Capital of Culture were pushed aside today — Saturday 7 July — since I'd just walked six-odd miles from Mdina, which sits imperially on a plateau in the south-west of Malta. Known as "The Silent City", I thought the old capital would be ideal while those in the new one — consumed by World Cup fervour — watched the England game. (Despite residing a hundred miles away from my father, Peter, I fervently trained it back to watch Liverpool and am still, eighteen months on from his passing, yet to view another footy match.)

I wasn't planning on walking only the queue for the bus mirrored that outside Oxford Street Selfridges on Boxing Day and I feared standing in the searing heat for an hour as single-deckers passed. Worst still was that tourists were streaming the quarter final on their gadgets while slurping cans of Cisk, the tasteless local beer. Together this made up my mind: I was walking back.

I subsequently left the queue before — given it was 34 degrees — lathering my face in factor 50. I rubbed in an extra couple of blobs, more out of necessity, but I'd like to think my sister beating skin cancer would compel me regardless of my face reddening quicker than a politician caught with his pants down. Standing on a hill, just outside the medieval walled city, I could make out Valletta's honey-coloured limestone walls — just. How hard could it be to navigate without a phone, I thought, since only fields appeared to stand largely in between?

I'd wanted to join a walking tour while in Malta but, being July, the season had all but finished. Now, though, I was about to embark on one of my own

– one not featured in any itineraries I read online. I soon understood why: roads aren't always accompanied with pavement.

The first (Telgha Tas-Saqqajja) is as soon as you walk eastwards from Rabat. I couldn't inspect what was growing in the lush-looking field on my right because I was continually ducking underneath tree branches to avoid encroaching too much into the path of oncoming traffic. Drivers were respectful, mercifully, with the only beeping coming from vehicles flying St. George's flags, though I didn't know at this point whether they beeped due to my quintessential Brit abroad, Casper The Friendly Ghost-like appearance or because the Three Lions had scored.

I'd left Mdina not long after arriving since I came across Saint Dorothy's Convent which reminded me of my late grandmother, Dorothy, the loss of whom I'm yet to register. (I'd likewise exited The Pub soon after entering given Peter bore a striking resemblance to Oliver Reed, photos of whom adorn the wall.) The first anniversary is a fast-approaching date I dread so much that I believed noisy Valletta would be preferable to Mdina's contemplation-inducing alleys. The distinct lack of pavement left no room for reminiscing, gratefully, concentrating my mind fully before (turning right onto Triq L-Imdina with its narrow and non-existent pavements) setting eyes upon St. Dorothy's Convent School.

The site's big, so big it has separate entry and exit gates, which meant I couldn't ignore it. There was an eerie silence with it being closed and the roundabout momentarily free of traffic. Suddenly – and surprisingly given their seasonal migration for breeding – a Robin appeared before perching upon a branch. The silence was punctuated by tweeting which, together with the sun on my face, reminded me of happy – happiest – times spent in Dot's garden listening to her budgies chattering, chirping and clicking. It took twenty-or-so seconds for tears to flow, only the second time since last August, but these where interpreted as running lotion by a groundsman with Popeye-size forearms and a jaw like Desperate Dan who was evidently bemused by my presence.

Standing on flat ground, I couldn't use the domed basilica peering above the ramparts or cranes as a guide. Sad, and disorientated by the low-flying aeroplanes above, I continued walking, hoping all roads leading to Rome went via Valletta. Suffice to say, they don't and, even though pavement was largely present for the remaining four-odd miles, no one appeared to use it apart from an emerald-green lizard. Thankfully, (re)construction work is ever-present as the Mediterranean island undergoes a makeover and thirty minutes later (in Qormi) I shouted up to a bricklayer on scaffolding.

Although I wasn't walking the Nile or Himalayas, I felt like Levison Wood when confirming my route towards The Phoenician, a hotel named after ancient explorers. Aside from walking up another pavement-less road (Triq Hal-Qormi), over well-manicured roundabouts and underneath North African-inspired wooden balconies, it was drama-free until the Law Courts, where protestors held a refugee solidarity demonstration in support of the humanitarian ship Lifeline. Sitting in Costa with my medium flat white (only small, alas, is available in the UK), an hour and forty-five minutes after leaving Mdina, I thought about the treacherous journey migrants were making. It reaffirmed how fortunate I was, not only geographically- but also grandmotherly-speaking, since not many are called 'My Pal' by a saint-like individual.

Only now, eleven months on from Dot's passing, did I subscribe to Tennyson's adage that it's "better to have loved and lost than never to have loved at all."

The Forgotten People
by Anu Devi

The deck of the Billabong Stilt House stretches several meters into the Celebes Sea off the coast of Mabul, Borneo, creating a spectacular space to view the turquoise waters. I am captivated by the marine life beneath, from the chocolate chip sea star to the turtle poking its head out to say hello.

With the 50x optical zoom of my camera, I decide to look for turtles from the deck. Suddenly, I notice a few people on wooden canoes trying to capture my attention.

"Money, money, baby," says a young girl. Accompanied perhaps by her sister, she holds a gondola-like rowing oar in one hand. With the other hand, she moves her fingers to her mouth to signal hunger.

"I don't have any money on me! Do you want some food?" I ask.

She smiles and nods!

On another canoe, a man picks up a large plastic bottle containing a foot-long mantis shrimp to sell. "Buy, tasty," he says. I wonder how he got the shrimp into the bottle and explain that I have no cooking facility. The instantaneous change in his facial expression tells the profound story of his survival needs, which disheartens me.

I give the man and the girls some food and watch them paddle away. Driven by curiosity, I zoom in with my camera to learn more about the girls.

The girls canoe towards a cluster of anchored boat houses, no more than five meters long and two meters wide. The boat houses are old and have a central structure that is covered with colorful sheets to keep the sunlight out.

I stand in shock and watch: four adults and four children are living on the small boat house. A child is playing on the roof with a wood. A lady is cooking, while two elders and a mid-aged man are sitting near with a baby. The girls attach the canoe to the boat house and carefully climb on. They show the food to the adults. I assume they are a family and work together to sustain themselves.

I look around the waters and notice several boat houses, each with its own family, its own story.

After this encounter, I attempted to learn more about these sea people from the local community on land as well as by doing some research.

I learned that they are the Bajau Laut people (also known as the Sea Gypsies). They are known for their free diving skills and ability to capture sea life from deep waters. Tourism has created another channel of engagement and trade for them. Interacting with visitors on stilt houses has become a routine and a source of income for them.

The Bajau Laut people are stateless. Decades ago, they settled on the water around Malaysia, the Philippines and parts of Indonesia. However, they are denied a nationality by the governments. They lack access to healthcare, education and jobs as they have no legal documentations. They rarely set foot on land, only when it is necessary to sell their catch, get fresh water or buy boat parts. Their children grow up just as their parents did.

The Bajau Laut are a minority group forgotten by the East and the West.

I wonder if the Bajau Laut people are happy.

I realize how easy it is to be a blind tourist and how much I take for granted!

Sea Gypsies

A Beach Walk in Phuket
by Syd Blackwell

The beaches of Phuket in the 1970s, had vast stretches uncluttered with tourism. One day while walking alone on one of those beaches, I overtook a couple. They greeted me cheerily, so I slowed my pace and joined them. They looked older than my parents. In months of travel in Asia, I had not seen any other travellers like them. Of course, I was curious to learn more.

I asked them where they were going.

"Australia", they quickly answered, in unison.

"When do you plan to get there?" I enquired, but they didn't know. And, thus began their tale of travel.

He had been a civil servant in England; she a stay-at-home mother. They had retired to a quaint cottage in Cornwall, just as they had dreamed and planned for so many years. After a couple of years, on a sun-dappled afternoon while they were reading books in the garden, he put his book down and asked his wife, "What are we doing?"

Somewhat nonplussed, she answered, "We're retired. That's what we're doing. We're being retired."

"No, no, that's not it", he quickly responded. "That is not what we are doing."

"Alright, then," she continued, somewhat exasperated, "just what are we doing?"

"We're waiting to die."

This stunning announcement led to a much-spirited discussion, but in a stunningly short time, a great decision had been made. They would sell everything, and they would go travelling. They had never travelled very far their whole lives. They had never even been outside Great Britain. On this particular afternoon, they had agreed that life as travellers was better than sitting around "waiting to die".

Naturally, their family and friends were shocked and dismayed and tried to dissuade them. But, this was not to be. They had made their decision. They were now travellers and they were going to travel to Australia.

By the time we walked together on that Phuket beach, they had already been on the road for fourteen months. Everything they owned was in their backpacks. They had traversed Europe and followed a traditional backpacker route through the Middle East and southern Asia, through countries not then violated and disrupted by greedy manipulations. They had been unencumbered by plans, schedules, or expectations. They just made it up as they went, adjusting to what they found, stopping whenever they wanted and leaving when it felt right. They told me they were in no hurry to leave Thailand. They wanted to see "the bridge on the River Kwai", and the ruins at Ayutthaya, and Chiang Mai, and maybe venture into the Golden Triangle, and visit Koh Samui, an island off the east coast of Thailand with a twelve-metre tall golden Buddha, that was not even on most backpacker itineraries. Australia seemed a long way away.

I reassessed my walking companions. Yes, they were certainly old, but I had failed to notice they were also lean, muscular, and well-tanned. In short, physically quite different than so many others of that era who were also in their late sixties. Undoubtedly quite different than what they themselves had looked like more than a year before.

I asked them why they had decided to go to Australia. They explained that Australia was the farthest away place they could imagine. (They weren't wrong by very much as the actual antipode to England lies south of New Zealand.) That seemed a perfectly reasonable response to me.

Then I asked them what they would do after they had reached their travel destination. They sort of avoided the question by telling me Australia was an awfully big country and it might take them quite a while to get around to various bits of it and that would give them lots of time to think about where they would next travel.

"So, you wouldn't think of staying there, in Australia?" I probed.

"Oh, we might for a while," he replied cautiously.

"But not long enough to be 'waiting to die'," she quickly added with a giggle.

We walked and talked a long time more, until I felt a wave was threatening to engulf me on that Phuket beach, a wave that would sweep me away with them to Australia. This couple, both well past twice my age, had enchanted me with their serendipitous travels and their unbound enthusiasm.

But I was westward bound and would soon be in Nepal. It was time for us to part. I wrote their names in my journal, but their English mailing address was in a country where they would never again belong. I knew I would never write. I knew we would never meet again.

Now, I am older than the English couple were on that Phuket beach. In the intervening years, I have often recalled that walk, thought about them, and wondered about their further travels. Today, of course, they would write a blog, and thousands, most of them complete strangers, would follow their footsteps. Then, there was just the moment, a spiritual sharing, an inspiration, that has travelled beyond the boundaries of lives.

Seaspray
by Robyn Boswell

The South Pacific runs deep in my veins. It's been the view from my windows, the place where I have spent many days of my life sailing its sapphire seas and camping on its sandy shores. The Pacific Islands feel like our backyard and I'm instantly at home there. Fiji was a perfect place for a family holiday. We spent a couple of days inhaling the scents and sounds of Suva, then drove very carefully across the rugged hills where a recent cyclone had scoured out the land and rolled boulders across the road. It was a much longer, more dangerous drive than we'd anticipated to our next hotel on the Coral Coast.

A photo on a brochure by the hotel desk leapt out at me instantly. Could it really be the Seaspray? As a teenager my favourite TV programme was 'Seaspray', which followed the crew of a sailing ship on their Pacific adventures. I had immersed myself in the crew's adventures, dreaming of one day sailing off to enjoy the freedom and adventure of a seafaring life. Now, here it was, the sailing ship of my dreams, offering day trips off the coast. I had to book a trip right there and then.

The morning of our sail to a resort on an off-shore island didn't dawn with a great deal of promise, with grey skies, but the gentle winds were just tickling the ocean into tiny waves and the weather was tropical-warm. We settled ourselves on the wooden benches lining the rails and cabin top, although it didn't take the two youngest members of our family long to discover the fun of flirting with the charming, fun-filled Fijian crewmembers down below in the saloon.

As we left the dock, we barely noticed a line of darker cloud smudged across the horizon; a harbinger of things to come. We've been at sea all our lives so weren't particularly worried. The sails barely filled as we slid out of the shelter of the harbour and relaxed into the voyage. As we sailed further out to sea, the dark clouds advanced and we enjoyed sailing at a much faster clip in gathering winds, until, like a shark attacking its prey, a sudden squall bit into us. The sails cracked as they took on the burden of the extra wind and the boat heeled over as the waves rose and the wind whipped frothy white caps off the top of them. It was exhilarating as the Seaspray took up the challenge, shook herself, heeled to port and tackled the waves. The rain hit next, dumping bucket loads of drenching water over the deck. The side curtains gave us a little protection, but we were slowly soaked in the spray drift and warm rain. The waves reared up further, slamming us from side to side. Some of the passengers began to discover that perhaps a large breakfast hadn't been such a good idea and down below in the saloon, sick bags were handed about as people began to panic and refused to come up on deck, which would have been a much better place for them.

My uncle and I, neither of us small people by any means, were sharing a wooden bench by the rail and opposite us, a young German woman huddled on a seat with her back against the cabin top. As a particularly large wave felt like it was about to tip us onto our beam-ends, there was a crack, our seat came adrift and began to slide across the deck towards the young tourist. All these years later I can still see the look of sheer horror on her face as we bore down inexorably on her, unable to get off our seat. I was certain we were about to smash her kneecaps. We were all powerless against the force of nature and fortunately just as we were about to crash into her, the next wave flung us in the opposite direction and we slid right back to our starting point.

We were revelling in the exhilaration of the wild sailing and the screaming winds and sea, although it was obvious, we were in the minority. Several of the crew were gathered on the deck, working the sails, whooping and hollering in the rain and making jokes about our passage through the reefs surrounding the islands. All of a sudden a few more crewmembers rushed forward. The big Fijians, who had been so full of laughter and fun, were suddenly serious as they gathered rapidly on the foredeck. The visibility was close to zero and they were all staring fixedly ahead of the boat. One climbed out on the bowsprit whilst a couple of others held tight to his ankles. They were all peering into the foaming mist that surrounded us and were looking decidedly worried. Suddenly one of them let out a huge yell and waved his arms frantically. The yacht tacked fiercely, almost ejecting us all from our seats on the deck. We looked over the side and no more than a few metres away was a marker buoy and waves slamming against a reef, snarling and white. Suddenly the whole adventure seemed a little less fun.

As tropical squalls do, it dropped away quickly, and we ended up motoring to our destination, somewhat damp and a little battered. The resort on the island did a roaring trade in t-shirts, but I suspect their food sales were down that day. We finished the trip with a sedate ferry trip back to the mainland, accompanied by the Seaspray crew who were back to their beaming, jocular selves.

I had a Dream
by Brigid Gallagher

My taxi deposited me at the old port of Skiathos, as the sun rose on a very COOL early October morning. I soon discovered that the next available ferry to Skopelos was due in SIX hours - a very long wait after three flights from my home in Donegal, Ireland!

I was living out my dream of visiting the islands featured in one of my favourite movies - "Mamma Mia."

Entering a small cafe, I spied some freshly baked pastries. "I'll try one of those please," I told the waitress, as I pointed to a spinach and feta pie or "spanokopita." Spinach, leeks, scallions and onions, feta cheese, eggs and fresh dill were wrapped in crisp filo pastry, producing a heavenly sensation on my tongue.

Happily replenished, I spent the remaining time *people watching*, including a large group embarking on a "Mamma Mia" themed sailing trip. "Dancing Queen" played on deck, as a series of scantily clad men and women stepped onboard. They were frozen! Indeed, one middle aged woman wearing a bikini and a see-through top, had the good sense to turn around and head back to her hotel. The others braved the unusually inclement weather. Once my own ship arrived, I climbed up to the passenger deck and entered a sheltered cafe with a view of the Aegean.

Unfortunately, nine days before my well-planned Greek Odyssey, I had learned that a freak three-hour storm had hit Skopelos. Walls had crumbled, houses and businesses were flooded, and a car park had literally fallen into the sea, along with cars, motorbikes...

The island was declared a disaster zone. What should I do?

I telephoned my accommodation on the edge of Skopelos Town.

"We have suffered no damage, and we are still open for business," my hostess assured me.

Finally, I arrived on my island paradise and I was greeted by a very welcome sign "Brigid," before being driven a short distance to a beautiful ground floor apartment, a mere 100m from the Aegean.

A short time later, I was lulled to sleep by the sound of the waves.

Skopelos is incredibly hilly and covered in pine forests. Thankfully, the walk into town took just ten minutes via flat but very muddy roads. Although the Greek army were doing a sterling job repairing roads and bridges, I learned that several cars remained in the harbour awaiting specialist lifting equipment. Sadly, it was unsafe to swim off Skopelos Town beach.

My long-held dreams of leaving my apartment and jumping into the ocean or the swimming pool had now evaporated, for I soon discovered that my hostess had told me a white lie, as her pool now lay filled with MUD!

Undaunted, I hopped on the local bus and spent a number of delightful sunny afternoons at Panormos Beach, where I swam in the open sea for the first time in a number of years.

I heard several local *yarns* surrounding the filming of "Mamma Mia," including the spotting of Strip and Pees (Meryl Streep and Pierce Brosnan) in a local bar. It reminded me of a similar Irish *tale* of a Hughdie Mc Menamy alias Yehudi Menuhin playing in a village pub in my home back in County Donegal.

My holiday would not have felt complete without a visit to the chapel of Aghios Ioannis, where Meryl and Pierce were married after climbing all 202 steep steps up a mighty cliff. I boarded the local bus to the island's capital Glossa, then hopped into a taxi for a ten-minute white-knuckle ride around very winding roads, which had not yet recovered from the mighty storm. I departed the taxi, ever thankful that I was the only tourist willing to make the climb that morning. I would not have wanted to attempt it in the busy high season.

Overcoming my fear of heights, I ascended the mighty rock, took out a song sheet and began to sing,

"I don't want to talk..."

My version of "The Winner Takes It All" was no match for Meryl's rendition, but I shed a load of emotional baggage on that Greek cliff!

Another hair-raising taxi ride later, I looked forward to a relaxing meal, before heading back to Skopelos Town. However, I did not anticipate a lunchtime cabaret with a difference.

It was the weekend of Staphylofest, the island's 3rd annual grape festival, and a loudspeaker announced that a salesman was in town. He produced fluffy bedspreads, rugs, a hairdryer, a saw, an umbrella... from the back of his van.

The hairdryer metamorphosed into an imaginary ear syringe, which he demonstrated to anyone willing to watch, amid peals of laughter. I felt reluctant to leave, as I pondered on Staphylofest's ongoing entertainment.

At holiday's end, I bade a very tearful farewell to the islanders, before setting sail to Skiathos. On the ferry, I caught up with Skopelos News blog, and discovered that the Greek Prime Minister Alexei Tsipras, and the Defence Minister Panos Kammenos, had flown by army helicopter to Skopelos Town football pitch, shortly after my departure.

They were reported as enjoying a brief lunch, surrounded by onlookers, before they inspected the remaining storm damage...

View from Aghios Ioannis

Stonemason
by Ronald Mackay

By the age of 12, cycling to youth hostels in my native Scotland had become my weekend passion. With my savings of ten shillings, I bought a neighbour's bike. He'd left school, started his apprenticeship at 15 and bought himself a bicycle with drop handlebars.

His old one suited me just fine. He'd looked after it well. Once I'd cleaned and oiled and rubbed and polished, to me that bike was the finest Raleigh in the whole wide world, with its Sturmey-Archer, 3-speed, hub-gear. With it came an old, canvas saddlebag. Everything I needed for the weekend squeezed into it – a tin plate, a fork-knife-and-spoon set, a bag of oatmeal, two tins of Heinz beans and two of macaroni and cheese, spare socks and clean underwear. A chipped enamel mug hung from the strap that closed the pocket that held my John Bull puncture repair kit and all-in-one box-spanner. My ex-army, cape-groundsheet was buckled on top by two leather straps for easy access because the rain would pound us at least once every hour.

A school-friend's father and mother had introduced five or six of us 12-year-olds to the Scottish Youth Hostel Association by generously inviting us on the 26-mile, each-way trip from Dundee to the stone Roundhouse in Glenisla. The Roundhouse had been built circular, we were told, because long ago, a sly tinker had once warned a Scottish gentleman that Auld Nick would catch him in a corner. In an attempt to outsmart the Devil, he had built himself a home without corners. Struck by the drama, we never thought to ask if the Roundhouse had worked as planned.

Soon, two school-friends and I graduated to longer trips with greater distances between the overnight stays in the hostels. Expert, we became, at planning, budgeting, packing and navigating from one simple hostel to the next. We also became expert at battling against headwinds, pushing our bikes up steep mountain braes, surviving on sugared tea, oatmeal, bread and treacle, and mastering the chores all hostellers had to perform before the warden would return your membership card and release you to pursue the next stage of your adventure.

One day, when pedalling into a drizzly head-wind in Caithness, we stopped to watch a stonemason at work in a bleak quarry. He had levered great slabs of rock from the quarry wall with an iron bar many times longer than he was tall.

We watched him examine a grey-green slab for long minutes as if judging a well-finished cattle-beast at a Highland Show. He'd walk around it, hand on chin, bright eyes searching. He'd ponder it from all angles, even getting down on his hands and knees to examine its underbelly. Determining its gender, perhaps?

Then he approached the board where the tools of his trade were laid out like cards ready for a game of patience – bull-set, point, mash, rock-pick, round hand hammer, stone-buster, cold-chisel. He selected two. The perfect combination of hammer and chisel for this job. He placed his cold-chisel just so and tapped it lightly with his stone-buster. A sheet an inch thick and twice the size of my bicycle separated itself from the mother rock, slipping off it like a domino from its stack. It lay there at a gentle angle. He lifted the grey-green sheet and gently laid it on its other side. We marvelled.

"Would you pe looking at that now! Two faces that none but us haff effer seen before this fery moment!"

He's looking lovingly at the revelation his skill had revealed. He's tracing his hand over the patterns left by the bones and shells of ancient creatures as if they offered the power to heal. Then he repeats his performance. Again, and again. Unhurried, lovingly, with reverence -- bringing the distant past alive before our young eyes.

"How do you do that?" I ventured.

"Once a man understants a rock..." He paused, caressing the thought, looking into infinity. "Once a man understants a rock, all he must too is tap her chently and she will open for him. She will open for him like the paches of your Bible!"

I looked at his eyes, heard the English words infused with his native Gaelic, and have never forgotten.

Snake in the Grass
by Dolores Banerd

It was December 2013 and just past eight in the morning when I emerged fresh-scrubbed from my air-cooled room at the Swastika Bungalows (actual name) in Sanur on the resort-island of Bali.

Of course, I'd also slathered my face and arms with sunscreen and donned my widest-brimmed straw hat. What I knew about Bali from a previous trip is that the sun would blaze pitilessly —the same as the day before and the day before that. What I didn't know was this could have been the last day of my life.

I was starting early in order to walk the 3-mile paved footpath by the beach before the unwelcome arrival of throngs of tourists, pushy vendors and the most intense sun. There are several short ways to reach it, but my favorite and most scenic was to cut through the luxurious Bali Hyatt resort, which was farthest from my guesthouse, but worth every extra step. I was fit so I had the "extra steps" in me and I was retired which meant I had all the time in the world. Or so I thought.

This Hyatt property had it all. It was immense—a 37-acre posh resort edging the ocean—and offered an abundance of amenities to please the pampered. It was also a feast for the eye, a modern-day Garden of Eden with a landscape filled with intimate pathways, shade-filled walks and glens, inviting swimming pools and serene secluded lily ponds. Best of all, as far as I was concerned, is that it was nestled in a splendidly ordered jungle teeming to the max with exotic flowers and thick with lush foliage.

All in all, an agreeable place and I was looking forward to my tramp through the acreage. However, to my surprise, as I approached its outer limits, I noticed it was more jungly than I remembered, so dense with vegetation it seemed impenetrable. And there was a darkness about it. It looked abandoned, and it was. Within minutes, I spotted large *No Trespassing* and *Keep Out* signs posted at intervals. Later, I learned that the property was closed for 18-months for an extensive renovation.

Still, it beckoned me. Despite the wildness of the terrain—Mother Nature was rapidly reclaiming it—I had my heart set on trekking through it (perhaps there's some Tarzan/Jane in my DNA). I was also confident I could get away with it because it was early in the day. I saw no one. Once I entered the property, no one would see me.

While mulling over my plan, I continued walking until I reached what had once been the main entrance. The paved roadway was torn up, but its outline was still visible. Ah, I thought, this is the perfect place to start my trek to the beach, but it wasn't. Just as I stepped a few feet inside the grounds, I noticed a uniformed Balinese Security Guard sitting on a single chair placed a short distance ahead of me. He was hatless. I particularly noticed his lack of a hat because, like most southern Californian women, I consider Enemies Number 1 and 2 to be UVA and UVB rays. In my mind's eye, I shook my finger at him for living dangerously.

My mood darkened, but not for that reason. His presence meant the managers of the Bali Hyatt were serious about the "No Trespassing" edict. Of course, I could have hiked through the property by entering where the guard could not see me but something (a Guardian Angel perhaps?) nudged me into abandoning my plan. When I hesitated, it practically screamed at me —*stop, don't be stupid, pay attention to the signs.* Luckily, I listened and gave up on the idea. Instead, I retraced my steps, and arrived at my destination, the beach footpath, by an easier route.

Two mornings later while lingering over a latte at an outdoor café, an icy terror gripped me as I read an article in the local English-language newspaper. It stated that two days earlier—on the same day as my aborted walk-through—the Security Guard at the Bali Hyatt had been strangled and crushed by a 15-foot Burmese python. According to eyewitnesses, after the brutal killing the python retreated into the thick vegetation. He was still at large.

I recoiled from the newspaper as if the serpent was slithering toward me.

After I caught my breath, I realized that had I persisted in my desire to tromp through the Hyatt's property I could have been the python's ill-fated victim and the news article would have read:

American Tourist Killed by 15-foot Python.

Early yesterday morning, two local citizens directed the police to the body of an American woman discovered on the Bali Hyatt property currently under renovation. According to the police, the (cough, cough) year-old woman was strangled and crushed by a 15-foot Burmese python that had been terrifying the local residents for weeks. Apparently, the female traveler had ignored the posted warning signs and was traversing the immense Hyatt property when she was killed. A local resident who witnessed the grizzly event stated that after the brutal attack the python retreated into the dense brush and has not been seen again.

I lingered over my latte for many more minutes awash in shock and grief. The shock was how close I came to putting myself in a dangerous situation. Had the snake and I crossed paths, I would have been a goner. You can't outrun a python.

After some of the horror subsided, I was overwhelmed with sadness at the security guard's fate and his family's loss. I felt especially foolish for inwardly chastising the man for his hatless status as he dutifully guarded the entry to the Hyatt. As it turned out, the danger he was in wasn't from the distant sun blazing down on him, but from the unseen deadly terror lurking so much closer in the thick grassy terrain.

All the World is a Stage
by Amy L. Bovaird

I had recently moved to the Middle East. As a newbie and still in the honeymoon stage of culture shock, I hadn't fully grasped how various traditions impacted everyday life in Ras Al Khaimah, one of the more traditional emirates in the Arabian Gulf. The rhythm of life in RAK—as it was called—was slow-paced, filled with camels and goats. Nothing like Dubai's superhighways or grandeur.

One Thursday night, "Broadway Baby" arrived in RAK. The singing troupe came from England and Scotland, other 'exotic' countries forming blips on my new radar screen. The expatriate community looked forward to the production. We were the second "city" on their six-week tour. I couldn't wait!

"Broadway Baby" would perform in the courtyard of the city's historical museum. Situated in an older section of Ras Al Khaimah, it hosted a variety of cultural programs and performing artists for the community each year. The open-air theater is nestled in the courtyard with a winding staircase behind it leading up to a natural stage, more befitting a Shakespearean drama than a host of Broadway singers. Nevertheless, with its palatial backdrop against the night sky, the museum bestowed such an air of expectation I'm sure both artist and audience felt the structure's allure.

That evening, I took my seat and eagerly awaited the start of the program.

The bald pianist wore full tails in spite of the near hundred-degree temperature. The female singers wore gowns with plunging necklines and the other men, their white dress shirts and tuxedo pants. They featured a medley of familiar songs from West Side Story to Gene Kelly's "Singing in the Rain" but their voices resonated like those in an opera.

I was beside myself in glory – enthralled.

About forty-five minutes into their presentation, the male lead took a deep breath, preparing to deliver a touching love song, no doubt. Just as he opened his mouth, the call to prayer sounded from the minaret of a nearby mosque. The performer looked up at the sky with a look of wonder. The *iqama*, a follow-up summons to prayer, engulfed the area. He looked around, waited for a minute. The distinct call seemed to fade away.

But we knew better.

When the singer opened his mouth again, the prayer call returned, louder and lasting longer. Laughter erupted. The entertainer turned to us, then to his fellow performers, clearly out of his element. Then he shrugged, sat down and picked up a large bottle of *Masafi* water, unscrewed the lid and took a long gulp. His fellow singers followed suit.

The production had come to a standstill! They smiled self-consciously at each other while initially, we, "the locals," watched them.

But then I noticed a shift in behavior.

"They're watching *us*," I whispered to Lesa, the librarian at the Men's campus.

"What else are they going to do?"

Some members of the audience pulled out books. Obviously, the unscheduled intermission didn't take them by surprise. Others left to walk around. Two young Emirati girls swung their long black hair from side to side in unison. They stepped to the right then to the left, and finally toward each other, catching hands. When they let go, they danced in opposite directions. Their floor-length *gallabeyas*, against the ground. I recognized the dance as The Hair Dance, typically performed by young Ermirati girls. These two were just killing time.

One performer pointed the little girl out to the other singers. They watched, seeming fascinated. One of the women on stage fanned herself – waiting and watching us with interest.

We had become the entertainment and they, the audience.

"I think they're waiting for a cue from us to re-start," I observed.

"They're in for a bit of a wait – to the 'tune' of fifteen minutes," the librarian quipped.

In time, Ed, our college director, gestured from his front row seat, signifying the prayer call had officially ended. The production resumed without a hitch. Afterward, Ed hosted a small, intimate after-performance party at his villa. My name was one of six lucky ones drawn from a hat to attend the party. Could life get any better?

I had the chance to mingle with the performers and discuss the unscheduled interruption.

They laughed and clapped each other on the back in amusement. One singer said, "We were actually warned in advance. But I guess we didn't really *believe* it would stop the show. When the prayer call came, it was so loud, we couldn't carry on. But it sure was fun watching you guys."

The Shakespearean quote came to mind. *All the world is a stage.* That sure seemed to fit the role reversal.

Chatting with the British and Scottish performers as well as hobnobbing with my director at his villa made me feel like I was brushing arms with royalty. The *hors d oeuvres* included a platter of fresh oysters with splashes of lemon. In my euphoric state, this dish seemed quite a delicacy. I had never eaten *any* oyster until that night.

If this was how my life would go in the Middle East, what an adventure I would have!

Escaping a Gulag
by Ben Stamp

A couple hours in, now acquainted with our three fellow travelers, was when we finally felt comfortable enough to ask: "What's with the suitcases?"

"Well, we just shoved everything into the biggest bag we had. Six months is a long time!"

"Six months?" I gasped. "But the Solovetsky Islands aren't that big. Are they?"

No, they weren't. But they'd be working at the monastery, and no more boats would be traveling back to the mainland for six months.

"What do you mean no boats? Six months? We're leaving in three days."

We weren't. We were on the last boat. The last boat for the next six months. Already two hours into a freezing vein of water, which soon would be a frozen one. Six months imprisoned on an island, an island that had been the site of one of the most infamous gulags in the Soviet Union.

Chains clattered.

A scream from here would never be heard. That's how Solzhenitsyn had described this place. These islands. These floating pieces of land piled with shipwrecked boats and stone towers, one slanted gust from crumbling. And I couldn't think of a better phrase to describe my feelings as we stepped off the boat, the boat which we didn't have enough money to go back on alone. The boat that was the last boat.

The boat.

Imprisoned. Sentenced to six months, on a remote island in the North of Russia, with three days' provisions and 2,000 rubles (~28 euros).

A scream from here would never be heard.

But one of our new acquaintances had given us hope: his brother had been living on the island already for two years. Perhaps he could get us back.

"Are you sure?" I asked, after our last hope echoed the words of his brother. Six months.

He nodded. Positive.

"Ben, what's he saying?" Vera's vocabulary consisted of Hello, Yes, No, Beautiful, and Bye. But occasionally Bye and Hello got mixed up. Like the same-colored toothbrushes in the bathroom. For her, Paka and Privyet might as well have been toothbrushes.

"He's saying the same thing. Six months." My Russian, while better, still wobbled around on skates, every once in a while catching a break and gliding gloriously. And then a turn would come.

The four hands waving goodbye meant we were officially alone.

We started where the brother had recommended. "Perhaps they have space." And then: a parting gift. "Good luck."

Here, blond-wood floors creaked, complaining to our feet. Here, the scent of cow manure, pungent pine and a bit of grandma's house dust swam around us. Here, too, silence dominated. But not from peace and tranquility, no—from submission, from harsh acceptance. Not the kind of silence that makes you smile, but the kind that makes you quiver, that makes you stand erect, and tall, and proper, as if a Lieutenant is approaching. Or a mass murderer.

Here was a place far from other places. A place one might go to forget about places. Or might be sent, to have them forgotten. As was the case with Solzhenitsyn.

A scream from here would never be heard.

"Privyet?" I informed someone, anyone, of our presence, searching up the stairs. In the stables of bleating goats. In the empty hallway. At the check-in counter and in the dining room and the next hallway.

"Privyet." A doughy-faced woman, missing a smile. Something she'd been missing for years. Her eyes shifted to Vera. "You no stay here. Employees of monastery. Men only. Across road"—her powerful finger pointed—"there wooden cabin. Ask."

She, unlike the brother, did not leave us with any parting gifts.

"Privyet," I greeted the man in a long robe examining the sky outside the wooden cabin. His long-chained cross glinted in the sun. A reminder what one can rely on in a place like this. A place where screams are never heard. "We sent by woman. There. You know if rooms? Here?"

He, too, pointed. Down a winding dirt road. A one-lane country road, lined by human-sized reeds, bending in the breeze. Cows seemed to roam free— although something limited their grazing, right? The water, maybe? The endless blue sheet tying nothingness to nothingness to more and more nothingness which went on and never ended and you thought you'd never escape this island this life this open-air prison. But the monastery: it watched over the island—four, five, six plump silver Hershey's Kisses rested atop its bleach-white columns. Golden scepters, the likes of which the pope might wield, protruded from the thin tips of the Kisses.

111

The log cabin at the end of the country road was the right place. We could stay there for free, for one night, the big man signaled with his stubby index finger. "Then you be on own," he said, using the same finger to instruct us, half-scolding us. The way our boat companions had when we'd admitted not looking into the ferry schedules.

When our time expired, we wandered the island, sleeping in a cheap tent, in the freezing, golden-leaved forest. We got lost back there, in the woods. The golden leaves beginning to fall, leaving muddied bronze stamps on the trails. We found a lake. We found a local shack selling salted fish and expiring cans of beans, ate lunch by the shimmering water, laughing. Until we had to return to our tent, money dwindling, like the branches' leaves. The silence, as promised, had become oppressive, muffling jolts of hope. *And the fisherman? They have to take the boats out, to fish, right?* No. They had stockpiled. *But planes! There's a landing strip.* Money like golden leaves, dwindling.

What were we going to do?

And then, one morning: a ray of light. Was it real? I crawled out of the tent.

Swords of heat, slicing through the cold. Our salvation.

The muddy trails dried. The invading cold retreated. The man from the lodge, where we'd stayed for free, found us.

This way, he motioned with his hand.

We ran after him.

Vera

112

Escaping a Gulag (Part 2)
by Ben Stamp

"Of course! Of course!" they boomed, opening a rift in the silence we'd drifted through over the past few weeks. One of the two men in the group tried to hide us beneath his armpits, under his bulky brown jacket. "Come, no one know," he whispered.

But there were rules: "I sorry. Too many people for tiny boat," explained the Captain. "You wait. When others on boat, we see."

Then: the waiting, on the dock, one long leg stretch from freedom, from the laughing and smiling stretching the faces of this group of pious Russians who'd just finished a three-day pilgrimage to one of their holy sites, the Solovetsky Islands, and were now leaving, without problem—it was then we saw the futility of steps towards freedom, if the final lunge is never taken. Staying in your tent, with the gooey mud mushing beneath your backs as you rolled over in your sleep and your money dwindling like the lemon-colored leaves falling from the poplars and being cold and shivering and afraid you'd never escape this island this cold this foreign, open-air prison. Staying there, in all that, would be the same as having made it this far and not taking that final lunge. Being cold, and shivering, and listening. Listening to the mud squish beneath your back. For a week. For two weeks. Watching the lemon-colored leaves twirl downwards and stick in the mud. Bronzing as the days went by. Wondering if you, too, would soon be like that lemon-colored leaf. Bronzed. Forgotten. Hopeless. Stuck in the mud that squished beneath your back as you rolled around, cold, shivering. For weeks.

Waiting on the dock was like this. Waiting on the dock was like twirling down from a limb you'd been hanging on for some time, wondering if the breeze would catch you before you splatted in the mud. And stuck there, forever. Bronzing.

"All right, come come," the captain acquiesced, his hand outstretched for us to take that final leg stretch, to metamorph into part of them—the jolly, laughing, leaving group. "But you hide until open sea. Yes? Understand?"

We understood.

And then we met her. Ludmila. Her name formed to her. As if *she'd* chosen *it*. A sky-blue platok swaddled her chubby face, like little blue riding hood, ostracizing a forehead full of curling ashen bangs.

We were now smuggled cargo, smashed between old Russian women, busting boiled potatoes, boiled eggs, fresh cut tomatoes and wild mushrooms mixed into deceivingly tasty salads out of Tupperware wrapped inside crinkled sacks.

"What her name?" the older little-sky-blue-riding-hood pleaded, using a much frailer woman's legs as cushions. Almost laying, to get closer.

"Vera."

Her face spoke before she did. "That Russian name!"

"She's so krasivaya," she continued, staring at Vera, her eyes gleaming with memory, wet with the past. Perhaps a daughter. Or a daughter that had been, before. "I'm Ludmila."

"Ochen priyatna. I'm Ben. And yes, she is beautiful," I agreed. Me, too, now gazing at her, filling with memories. The tent, the twirling leaves. The squishy mud. Now it would be a story. Our story.

The small boat spit and popped into action, gurgling water, as we crawled away from the dock. The pink horizon melted, on the milky, smooth water out the submarine windows behind our heads. Long wrinkles tightened in the sheet of brightening silk behind us, opening.

"I sing her song," Ludmila declared.

Five Russian ballads later, Ludmila having closed her eyes and touched her chest, then Vera's chest, in multiple songs, as if to say, you don't need to understand the words: feel them—after all that, we inched across the open sea, the back-end sagging into the water, ten people over capacity. A trail of white diamonds on the choppy water, left behind by the sun, led to a hazy island. And after the captain ducked his head into the small wooden door where we were smashed between these women and said we could come out now, we could come out of hiding, we saw the trailhead of the white diamonds beaming on the sleek silver railing, glittering where we discussed life and love and religion, with Ludmila.

Me translating, Vera nodding, asking me to ask.

And, like that, discussing love, life, religion, with Ludmila, who'd only been one of many hands inviting us onto a boat, exactly two hours ago—like that, we distanced ourselves from the silent scream of the Solovetski Islands. From the shrinking promises of religion. From the soon-to-be-leafless trees, wooden fingerprints against the marmalade skyline. Harbored from the islands' ambient past, by the warmth of a Ruskaya dusha.

The same Russian soul which had steadied its flame in Solzhenitsyn, too, during his imprisonment on these very islands. A stay which had reminded him what's left after all else is stripped away: "know languages, know countries, know people."

And for the first time in weeks, no longer trapped, certain of not being stuck in the cold, and the shivering, and the mud, on an island off which we'd been told no boats would depart until summer, six months from when we'd arrived, for the first time since then, we hugged and took photos with "others who were alive, who were traveling [our] road, whom we could join to [ourselves] with the joyous word 'we.'"

Ben

Pago Pago
by Helen Bing

Fa'afafine or Faafetai?

When something gets lost in translation!

Different countries, different language and different cultures are the things that make travelling interesting. If everything was the same as at home, then what's the point of travelling.

As a nation, New Zealanders tend to be drawn to other places, often to find out more about their own roots, or out of curiosity. For those of us who live in the northern parts of New Zealand, we are lucky to live with people from a wide number of different ethnic backgrounds. Naturally, we also have a high Pasifika population, so, when our ship docked in Pago Pago, in American Samoa, there really was a feel of home for me.

When we dock in a new place, I like to get up on deck early. This day was no exception. The wharf lay below us. People were getting ready to set up the market place that was for our benefit. Huge bags of colourful t-shirts and lava lavas were being hauled out of cars. Bright shirts with flowers of the islands were waving in the wind. Beautifully woven bags and baskets were laid out on tables ready for the onslaught of tourists.

Beyond the gates that would lead us out into the real world the island rose up towards the sky. A pathway could be seen up through the bush to a memorial that was on top of the mountain. One of our friends had already decided that would be a great place for a bit of a run. At the base of the mountain were the trees where the fruit bats were hanging and screeching out to one and other. Every so often they would suddenly take flight, then settle back down in the trees.

Time for breakfast. We poor half-starved passengers like to make sure we are not going to faint with hunger! Over breakfast I check out the "Daily Planet" (my name for the newsletter that is put in our cabin each evening telling us the next day's activities) to see what's on the agenda for the day.

As we are in port, there's a brief history of the island, places of interest and useful phrases. This is about the time I let out a bit of a snort, have another look to see if I'm seeing right, then burst out laughing.

Talofa lava - hello. That's fine.

Fa'afafine - thank you.

Oops! Last time I heard, that was the name given to what is known as Samoa's third gender.

Well I carried on with my breakfast, as you do, then thought I had better make my find known. I had this vision of some people having quite an interesting day if they used their handy language guide, so, down to the reception I went.

"Good morning, Madam," I was greeted with by a young lass behind the counter.

Me, "Good morning. Is the "Daily Planet" written up on board?"

Young lass, "No ma'am, it's all done from head office."

"Well," said I, "there is a mistake here. They've put fa'afafine for thank you, and that means..."

"Do you speak Samoan, Madam?

"No, no," say I, "but in the school where I teach, we have a lot of Samoan kiddies, and you do pick up some key words."

Sceptical look from the young lass. "Madam, if you take this piece of paper, can you write it all down."

"Certainly." And off I go with my piece of paper and the pen she also thought to give me.

Well time ashore is precious, and by now it was a bit late to let the passengers know there was some dodgy translation on their sheets, so it wasn't until later in the day that I sat down with my iPad and Mr Google to check and make sure I hadn't got it all wrong. But no, I was right.

Fa'afafine - 3rd gender - a male raised as a female. Faafetai - thank you.

I wrote it all down and I took it back to the desk. There was a different girl on this time. I guess the first one had gone ashore to practise her Samoan. When I explained what it was all about, she just burst out laughing - and did anything come of it? I've no idea. But if you happened to have been in Pago Pago that day, and wondered why you were getting funny looks, this could be the reason why.

The Skelligs, 13/6/93
by Mike Cavanagh

Ragged, towering rock islands off the south-west coast of Ireland. Abandoned now, from the 6th to 12th centuries they were a monastic colony of which now only remains their stone-corbelled houses, chapel and ruined walls. While the only permanent residents now are seabirds, in summer tourists arrive on Skellig Michael, as did I in 1993, hoping for fine weather for the views, to see these islands in their clear glory.

Instead it was cold, grey, windy, raining, visibility down to tens of metres. Scrambling up the hundreds of hand-wrought stone steps to the half dozen 'beehive huts', I looked across to where Little Skellig was and couldn't even see past the low, ruined stone wall ten metres in front of me.

I took shelter in the gloom of one of the huts, the wind moaning, the rain chattering, my despondency growing. Then it dawned on me: how many days just like this had those ascetic monks put up with over the centuries? Wasn't this more 'real' than some picture-postcard views and beguiling summer light-dappled, calm ocean?

Here then, my homage to The Skelligs, and those who were there a long, long time before me.

* * *

"Ah, the wretchedness of it all, Father! We can sail no closer, though the very spray is upon our faces!"

(I)

Listen!

...asylum inviolate,
silence and space;
Listen!

as if it always
was,
always, both here
and

somewhere else.

Listen!

...the drumming of
senseless seas dreaming
rude isles in their midst;
the soundings of seabirds,
their scrimshawed calls becry the opening skies;
and the sighing of stone
ever
beneath the waves tolling,
beneath the birds wheeling,
beneath the calloused sky...
     - oh, but only, only

just!

Listen!

...a million feathered flights,
tumbling over countless fish filled meals;
a hundred million years of mineral twistings,
and a thousand years of sedentary, stoic dreams;

and ever, beneath the voices of
the vagrant squalling winds,
ever the sloughing ocean
ever the challenging sea
ever crying its rightful claim

true heart
     lone rock.

Listen!
for it is passing;
passing, still,
as always

(II)

Lulled and counter sunk
this counselled altar,
raised to the enigmatic dreaming of simple men;
aspirings steeped in the rocky beds
deep beneath
both the grieving and the worship,
and seeping from the ascension of these scars
crabbed into the island's flank,
carved into the island's flesh
and proffered to the glory
in the patient footfalls
of these
stooped and simple,
men

the glory,
and the worship
steeled in the journey's charge
of mortality's vigilant imaginings,
eked out of shivered stones
and plundered puffins,
the smells of musty seals
and guano's stench;
the archaic light that still is strung
through the needle's eye,
and cast upon the chapel of St Michael

like a blind man's thread
like a gannet's plunge
like a reclamation

      bene
          dictus

      blessed
          rock.

(III)

And over the while that men have slept
the years have fretted
fleet across
the surging, churlish waters;
till rushing now the pilgrims come
trading idols
not of salted skies
not of brazen winds and cracking seas
both purposeful and crazed,
but those, wrapped within these lambent days
and calm enrapturing rock walled bays,
as can be embalmed in postcards and little boxes and
spirited away...

though, strangely still,
dispossessed and hungering
to step
dry shod,
upon the nakedness of
rock and monotheistic memories alike;
seeking that which is momentous;
if only
momentarily

and still there is this guiding silence

    these clowning birds

    ...these wheeling,
wheeling cries...

and still,
as wind and wings above,
and fish and whale below, glide by,
still the deeper,

silence clings;

still the deeper still

     than that

As the passage of one age is made,
so the passing of one wave,

and time's ocean blithely swirls
around one more randomly
located obstruction.

(IV)

Lone rock –
at the true edge of the world suffers still a subtle siren
who beckons most to the straining heart
     and the tillered soul,
who beckons most to men such as these
who believed in miracles,
believed indeed in the indulgences of
time,
believed in their deeds the piety
of raging against the endless litanies
of oceans, winds and rains...

and in the beckoning,
in the supple shifts of time,
in the fey and feckless seas,
in the stark abyssal dreaming,
will be the bending, at the end of all things,
of even such faiths as these,
bedrock truthed,
birthed and anchored

as will all things be, in turn,
turned,
seduced and
finally sundered
from the bind of earth;
the absolution of time

all
to be beguiled by nothing more,
or less, than
the Iscariot kiss
and the lover's sigh
in the falling of
a drop of water
in the blink of time's
eye

bene aqua
      bene aqua
holy holy
      falling water

(V)

                    In nomine patre,
          here and all that remains of us,
                      et filii,
            as the rocks remember us,
               et spiritu sanctu,
        and all our ghosts when gone.

(VI)

Listen!

      in the winds
both the lamenting
and the glorying

                as it ever was as it ever shall be

Listen!
      in the rains
both the striving
and the futility
                as it ever was as it ever shall be
Listen!
      in the oceans

the raging and the silence,
the damnation and humanity,
the exultation, and the stark humility

            as it ever was as it ever shall be

Listen,
you wretch of the wester-wind,
scion of the torn-sky's dawning...

for above every stoic rising
it is calling;
below every root sunk to seek the core;
within every moment of defiant silence
it is calling;
behind every watching from dusk to dawn

that which itself has no power,
cannot be seen,
that which forever has no meaning,
that which cries out
to draw you yet under,
to draw you yet down;
cries to drown even you,
in your proud, silent abandon,

cloud-thorn crowned
         and
             bloodied
rock

          oh yes,
even you...

                       bene infidelitas
                       bene solitarius
                       bene infidelitas

omnia semper in tempore.

The Day I Disappointed the Queen
by Apple Gidley

I am a fortunate woman, and at times, an opinionated one. I have criss-crossed the world since aged one month. Not surprisingly, those earliest experiences of flying to Nigeria are non-existent in my memory bank. I do remember my first global circumnavigation - Singapore Perth Sydney Fiji Tahiti Acapulco Mexico City San Juan Beef Island Antigua London Rome Columbo Singapore. It was a lot of flying, and though owning my own blue passport and the corresponding blue BOAC Jet Club book I was not responsible for their safe keeping.

Then I was.

Travelling solo from age ten to and from Malaysia and Australia, then from Papua New Guinea, in the name of education, I became adept at negotiating both immigration and customs. I knew the value of that regal blue passport. My mother had told me I was to be extra careful because it belonged to Her Majesty, The Queen. It, and she, would guarantee me, and all those whose privilege it was to carry one, safe passage.

The preciousness of that blue book was ingrained in my psyche. Though as I reached the ripening age of fifteen, I became less diligent at getting the captain to sign the other - the by then defunct BOAC book. British Airways now ruled the stratosphere. To my almost-adult mind it was so juvenile. And yet, here I am today, at sixty, looking up that very book to confirm the aforementioned flight path.

Fast forward many years and I became a guardian to those who held the now plum-coloured passport that declared membership of the European Union. It did still have the lion and unicorn holding the crown aloft. It did not though have the same feel. That somehow irrevocable belief that entry would be given upon its proffering. There were an increasing number of citizens from an increasing number of countries to whom the burgundy book was issued.

However, I took my guardianship seriously. I was living in a small despotic country tucked into the fold of every atlas - Equatorial Guinea in West Africa. I was Her Britannic Majesty's Honorary Consul reporting to the British Ambassador in Cameroon.

One of my roles was to ensure every British subject was registered. Should civil mayhem erupt I would know who was who, and who was where. It was also my job to reclaim said burgundy passports should an over-zealous government official confiscate one. I used the very words my mother taught me. In poor Spanish, I would remind the man behind the scarred desk under a fan rotating so slowly flies could still land on it, that the passport in question did not belong to Mr John Smith. It belonged to The Queen. Her name always spoken in capitals.

Another role was to ensure DBNs - Distressed British Nationals - who for whatever reason imprisoned, were at the very least not being harmed and preferably, if the infraction was trumped up or minor, were released forthwith. More often than not release was relatively straightforward. More often than not it was suggested, either by me or the authorities, that the detainee might like to leave the country sooner rather than later. With his plum passport.

A passport, whatever the colour, is a thing of beauty when faced with detention. It is not advisable to allow it to go through a wash cycle or be taken for a swim no matter how inviting the cobalt waters. Nor indeed should it be lost. Something that happened with alarming regularity to people who did not have the benefit of the same parental warning.

I was, during those Equatorial Guinea years, frequently travelling back to England due to my mother's failing health. She lived deep in the Somerset countryside. I would leave Pitney at 2 am, allowing plenty of wiggle room for my drive to London Heathrow, in time for the red-eye flight to Zurich, from where I would board the plane to Malabo.

This particular trip, having returned the hire car, and taken the shuttle bus to the terminal, I was delighted to find a darkened, secluded bench on which to stretch for an hour or so. Wrapping my computer case around the luggage trolley then my wrist and, ever mindful of my passport, tucked my handbag under my head and promptly feel asleep.

Thump. My head bounced. Through the fug of disturbed slumber came the realisation, 'I've been robbed'. Galvanised, I untangled myself from the rest of my luggage, leapt over a rail and ran through the automatic doors in time to see red tail lights disappearing into the warren that is Heathrow.

My passport. My ticket. My wallet. My phone. All neatly bundled into one receptacle - a cornucopia of possibilities for the light-fingered.

The men-in-blue were wonderful, offering succour and tea, though bourbon would have been preferred.

"Do you know your passport number, Mrs Gidley?"

126

"How about your husband's phone number?"

"Your daughter's?"

"Anybody's?"

Answering a consistent 'no' I could however confirm my sister's address.

"Oh, that's grand," said the sweet, ruddy-faced copper, as if he'd won the jackpot. "We'll have a panda car stop around and get her okay to pay for a taxi."

The police graciously handed me into a hansom cab, assuring the driver I was good for the fare. All I had to do was beg the Foreign Office for approval of an expedited passport and obtain a new visa.

That was the day I learnt it doesn't matter what colour one's passport. The only way around entry into Equatorial Guinea, unless one was American, was with a large slice of humble pie. (US citizens not requiring visas due to the deal made between a US oil company and the Equato-Guinean government.)

Later that evening, sipping bourbon at my sister's kitchen table, I telephoned my mother who despite being vague about current events, either familial or global, commiserated with the words, "Oh sweetie, The Queen will be so disappointed."

Metaphysics in the mountains
by Celia Dillow

'Are you heading for Christ, *Señora*?', asked the border guard who controlled the tunnels. His uniform was dusty and aggressive, but he smiled with the smile of the mountains. Briefly surprised by the question, I said that yes, we were. He warned us that we had a long and difficult way ahead and that we should follow the road carefully. Then he waved us through his checkpoint.

We headed up the famous *Ruta Nacional 7*. It is a road of myth and magic which follows the old trade route through the Andes. Linking Chile's Pacific coast and the Atlantic edge of Argentina, it was used to bring gold and silver out of the mountains. Now, meat and leather and cereals are exchanged but there is a feeling of history about it. International road freight thunders through tiny frontier towns which are thick with the memories of warrior ghosts and generals. In 1817, General San Martín used this treacherous and unexpected route to cross the Andes and take the Chilean leaders by surprise. His journey lasted three weeks and he lost a third of his men along the way. Their audacity is woven into Argentine story and song and celebrated throughout the land.

In the high Andean passes the road climbs to nearly 4000m; it is a place of bright, white peaks, endless sky and fiercely cold night. The many-coloured rock changes in the light, striped with peach, lilac and aubergine. Mount Aconcagua, the highest mountain on earth outside the Himalayas, stands sentinel in the rare air where the condors turn.

We took the narrow way: an old, zig-zaggy section of the road which has been superseded by the new tunnels. Our road was rocky. The tyres skated on the unsealed surfaces as we avoided the deepest ruts. Fine, pink dust filled the car and the road twitched back and forth through dozens of sharp hairpin bends. It was a slow, terrifying climb. Guanaco nibbled and picked at the ragged edges of the tracks. They watched our clumsy passage and then skipped away, their ginger-cream coats fading into the landscape.

A few kilometres further up, we met some eager, dusty boys.

'How far are we from Christ?' we asked them, exhausted.

'Not far, *Señora*, but it is a very difficult and narrow way, you may miss the path. You must be sure where you are going'. They warned us to be careful and offered to sell us water.

The bronze statue, *Cristo Redentor de los Andes* (Christ the Redeemer) is on a high mountain pass at the border between Argentina and Chile. It is 3,800m above sea level, stands over 12m high and weighs 3600kg. It travelled from Buenos Aires by train and was carried up the mountain road by mules before being reconstructed on the border to celebrate the end of hostilities between the two warring neighbours, in 1904.

We gazed on Him, but he kept his eyes fixed along the frontier. On either side of Him, the bright flags of Argentina and Chile snapped and snagged at each other in the raw wind. If the peace treaty is ever broken, the mountains themselves will crumble to dust. It says so on the plaque at his feet. We scrambled to the highest point of the pass in the thin air and soft, mountain light. The vast landscape was of ice and rock: tongues of glaciers and the crazy, curvy road spooling down to the valley. The great altitude made our heads reel and our chests pound, but the peace was powerful. Like us, the other visitors moved slowly and murmured softly, preserving the silence of the space. Vendors, selling thick, sweet hot chocolate and *alfajores*, huddled against the wind and spoke in subdued voices. The smell of the chocolate hung, like incense, on the air.

We sat and waited for our hearts to stop thudding. Breathing deeply, we dragged the mountain air and mountain peace into our lungs and let our thoughts unwind. When it was time to go, we took our leave. His right hand was raised in blessing.

On our careful way down the mountain, the checkpoint guard asked,

'And where have you come from today, *Señora*?'

'We've come from Christ', I replied as we rattled back along the narrow way.

Andes

Aye Aye Captain
by Malcolm D. Welshman

For a brief moment on board, I change from being a guest speaker to Captain of P&O Cruises ship, Oceana, as it sails round the Western Mediterranean. It's a formal evening so I'm in black tie and consider I look debonair as I stroll through the glittering atrium of the ship, stopping to enquire of a couple of elderly ladies sipping G and Ts whether they are enjoying their cruise. Both nod enthusiastically. One looks up and says, 'You must be very proud of your ship.' To which her companion, with a beaming smile, adds, 'And you've such a lovely crew.'

There's a double take the following morning when they bump into me wearing jeans and tee shirt. But I make amends after lunch, escorting them slowly with their walking sticks to the far end of the ship and the Starlights Lounge where I'm giving my third talk about my experiences as a vet. Having ushered them into seats in the front row and commenced my talk, they promptly nod off.

Mealtimes as ever are fun. Freedom dining means meeting new people every time I enter the Ligurian Restaurant. The High Court judge travelling the world to advise on immigration. The postman based in Barnsley – a courteous, effete gentleman who has chatted up the lady next to me and then stands up when she is about to leave the table only for his trousers to fall down as he had unbuckled his belt during the meal. And the tall, sassy, blonde on board with her father, who buys six pairs of sling-backs in every port and who ditched her husband – though not her shoes – on her last cruise, flying back midway through it.

At one breakfast, I sit opposite a farmer and his wife. The talk inevitably turns to animals and what pets we each have. The moment arrives when the farmer pulls his phone out of his pocket.

'Here's pic of my pet,' he says, handing the phone across to me.

I find myself staring at a head-shoulders-and-horns shot of a Jersey heifer. A pretty picture indeed. Handsome. And so, I say.

The farmer nods enthusiastically. 'Certainly, better than the old cow sitting next to me.'

The look his wife gives him could have curdled a pint of that Jersey's milk within seconds.

I decide to offer my services as a tour escort. On a boat trip across Lake Bracciano in Italy, an elderly passenger trips and falls on deck and cracks open his forehead. As he comes to, I whisper to him that if he is able to miaow then perhaps I can attend to his wounds. That quickly revives him.

Introducing myself to the Spanish guide taking us on a shore excursion round Alicante a few days later, I mention that incident, adding that, on escort duty for a walking tour of Bergen, I'd lost my group twice; while on a trip up Mount Vesuvius, a gentleman in my tour group gashed his thigh, blood pouring down his leg. I don't appreciate all this has been said with the PA switched on. Everyone on the coach has been listening in. So, when I turn to introduce myself as the escort for today's trip, the passengers cower back in alarm at this harbinger of bad news in their midst.

I tend to prance around the stage while I give my presentations and in my last talk of the cruise, stepping backwards to the lectern, the ship gives a slight lurch. This sees me sailing past my laptop and disappearing behind the curtains, arms flailing.

Truly, I'm all at sea.

Now the Captain would have never done that!

Tent Pegs and Poles
by Susan Mellsopp

In absolute frustration I crawled out of my warm sleeping bag and crept up behind my eldest son. I snapped the headphones against his ears. Looking at me with absolute disgust he demanded to know why I had done that. His out of tune singing night after night was keeping us all awake and I had finally exacted some hilarious retribution.

I had never been camping as a child, but after reading a book about a young couple who cycled around the world pitching their tent wherever the mood took them, I was hooked. Farm responsibilities meant my children had never had a proper family holiday, tenting offered an affordable solution.

A decision was made to travel around the East Coast of the North Island, a place full of lonely but beautiful beaches, magnificent bush walks and friendly small rural communities. Borrowing an old-fashioned square scout tent, I soon discovered it had no floor. Rules were swiftly devised – the naughtiest child had to fill in the toilet we dug at each free remote camping site and help pack the tent. After staying in small coastal towns where old Maraes, early wooden churches and huge pohutukawa reigned, we finally relaxed. Swimming several times a day became the norm; in the icy Motu river with our car parked in the stony riverbed, in rolling surf on deserted beaches and in sheltered inlets.

We spent several hours enjoying the infamous town of Ruatoria where the main mode of transport was a horse. The local radio station blared its message of national defiance everywhere. Asking a local farmer if we could camp in his paddock next to the beach, he readily agreed for the sum of $10. I had, much to the family's annoyance, brought a banana box full of library books to read. I slept and read all day while the children ran wild exploring the beach, the surrounding dry hills and climbed trees. Showering under a freezing cold waterfall was exhilarating. We swam in the blue Pacific waters and ate fish caught just 10 minutes earlier.

Arriving in Tolaga Bay a change of diet was essential. Meals had consisted mainly of cornflakes, bread and packets of rice risotto padded out with cauliflower, courgettes and tomatoes purchased at roadside stalls. The smell of the local fish and chip shop was irresistible. I ordered fresh snapper and chips which arrived wrapped in many layers of newspaper. Eating our greasy treat sitting on the long wharf with our feet dangling over the edge was fun until one of the children spotted a sea snake in the water and pandemonium ensued. Returning to our tent at dusk a noisy rustling and snorting greeted us. I shook the tent and a terrified half-grown wild pig emerged with a fresh lettuce in its mouth. The following night further rustling woke us. Not a pig but a curious large hedgehog was searching for food.

Nearing Gisborne, the only large town on the East Coast, we were all rigid with excitement, civilization! Our dreams were short lived. After two weeks living rough, we could not cope with the bustle of busy clean people and the overwhelming noise. After a quick trip to the supermarket then the bakery for fresh bread and melt in the mouth doughnuts full of real cream we were back on the road.

Mahia was a haven of peace and tranquillity. Situated in sand dunes among pine trees, we put up the tent away from other campers. The children roamed freely, often returning only for tomato sandwiches, baked beans or the inevitable rice risotto. I have never purchased this delicacy since. A group of louts, denied entry by the proprietor of the camp, decided to exact revenge. At 2am they set fire to pine needles around the perimeter and soon there was a thick smell of smoke in the air. Unable to wake my eldest son, eventually I screamed fire and shook him violently. Leaping up he grabbed a shovel and became the hero of the night as he poured sand over the fires.

Reluctantly turning towards home, we headed for Lake Waikaremoana. Erecting the tent in a free Department of Conservation camping area, curious kiwi rustled and called each other around our tent all night keeping us awake. Dishes and children were scrubbed in the clear fast running icy river. Miles of remote bush tracks became our playground as we explored deserted silent lakes.

Camping holidays became a way of life. We purchased a large three bay tent, Antarctic weight sleeping bags, a two-ring gas cooker and toaster. We travelled to Northland to visit the places of importance to our colonial history and spent four weeks camping around the South Island. A Victoria Cross recipient allowed us to stay on his farm, and my daughter was almost killed by a hooligan driving at high speed through a camping ground in mid-winter. I woke to water lapping over my air bed at a pony club camp. Our son was bashed over the head with a spanner by his frustrated travel weary sister. He was indignant when I took him into the ladies' toilet to clean up the blood. Our tent was filled with vomit by a sick child on a stormy night as the high winds sucked the tent in and out, despite it being tied to our car and nearby trees high in the Rimutakas.

Amazing people became instant friends. This included a police officer from Chicago camping in the West Coast wilderness just days after shooting a man during a violent robbery. We sat with him in the silence, trout disturbing the lake surface as curious native birds flew around us. We visited Havelock where Ernest Rutherford attended school and made a mercy dash for medical help to treat a child covered in mosquito bites. Camping was fun, hard work, rewarding and cathartic. It offered my family a window into the extraordinary remoteness of this beautiful country.

Lost in Transition
by Lindsay de Feliz

In 1964 we moved to Singapore when my navigator father was deployed to Seletar Air Force base. The family consisted of him, my mother, me, aged 8, my five-year-old sister and my two-year-old twin brothers.

Fast forward 18 months and I had passed my 11 plus at Seletar Junior School; although I was only 10 and was ready to go to grammar school, the only ex-pat grammar school was too far away from where we lived. It was decided that I should return to the UK, live with my grandparents and attend the local school in Purbrook, Hampshire where they lived. They came to Singapore for a holiday and in August 1966 I flew back with them. This time we flew BOAC and I was admitted to the BOAC Junior Jet Club and was the proud recipient of my log book and badge.

Christmas approached, and my grandmother told me that my Christmas present would be a trip back to Singapore to spend Christmas with my parents. Much as I loved living with my grandparents, I was overjoyed to be going to where I called home. The ticket was booked with BOAC, a special stewardess was organized to look after me on the flight, I put my pin on my jacket and my log book in my new handbag. We arrived at Heathrow to discover that BOAC had decided to go on strike, but I had been rebooked onto a Qantas flight which was going to Sydney, but I would get off at Bangkok and change to a Malaysian Airways flight to Singapore. The only problem was that there would be no special stewardess to look after me, and I had only just turned 11. What to my mind was worse was that there would be no entry in my BOAC Junior Jet Club log book. My grandmother said she would call my parents to tell them the change of arrival time and airline.

We took off and I was sick. I was sick every time we took off and every time we landed. The first stop was Rome, and everyone had to get off the plane and sit on hard plastic chairs in a transit hall. Next stop was Cairo, sick again, same chairs, then Bahrain, then Calcutta and finally Bangkok. Night was falling as we reached Bangkok and I wasn't really sure what I was supposed to do but I knew I had to get another flight. We went through immigration where the desk was about five feet tall. I was only four foot nothing but by standing on tiptoes I managed to push my passport onto the desk and then marched purposefully through the airport asking everyone where the Malaysian Airways desk was as I had no idea how to get the next flight. It seemed to take forever to find it and when I got there I was told my flight had left. The next one was in eight hours' time, so they booked me onto that. I asked them to call Mum and Dad to explain but they said they couldn't.

I had no money, so I couldn't call my parents, nor could I buy food. I wandered around the terminal asking anyone who had a friendly face if they could help me, buy me food and contact my parents. I did manage to get some food but that was it. Eventually I gave up and I returned to the ubiquitous red plastic chairs bolted to the scuffed tiled floor to wait, returning to the Malaysian Airways desk every 30 minutes or so to see if the plane was ready to depart.

Meanwhile in Singapore my parents had gone to meet my flight and I was not on it. They had no idea at all where I was. Had I stayed on the Qantas flight and gone to Sydney? Had I disembarked in Rome, Cairo, Bahrain or Calcutta? Had I been kidnapped in Bangkok? They were beside themselves and my father made numerous phone calls to airports across the world with no result. I was simply nowhere to be found. The only thing my father kept telling my mother was that I was sensible, and he was sure whatever the issue was I would sort it out. Eventually he discovered that I was on the next flight and they went back to Paya Lebar airport to meet me, where they received the news that the plane I was on was having difficulties and preparations were being made for an emergency landing.

Back in Bangkok I had eventually boarded the plane having been upgraded to First Class as I was rapidly becoming a Diplomatic Incident. The middle-aged gentleman sitting next to me was Dutch and he kindly lent me his handkerchief as I sobbed with relief when the plane took off for the first stop, Penang. Then I was sick.

I slept almost immediately and when I woke up, I asked the Dutchman if we had landed in Penang and somehow, I had slept through it? He told me we could not land as the landing gear was stuck.

We approached the airport in Singapore with everyone bracing themselves for a crash landing and as we hit the tarmac you could see flashing lights of ambulances and fire engines speeding alongside. In the end we juddered to a halt. I handed yet another full sick bag to the stewardess and undid my seat belt, desperate to see my parents but not sure if I would be shouted at for having put them through so much worry. One can never tell with parents. The pilot asked everyone to remain seated while a VIP left the plane. That was me! I was escorted off the plane, into a black limousine and whisked off to a private room in the terminal where Mum and Dad were waiting. And they didn't shout at me.

Me – aged 10

One Day in Canada – A Journal Excerpt
by Syd Blackwell

Thursday, June 20, 2013

We woke before 8:00 in our wonderfully comfortable, rustic bed in a private guest room in Jasper, Alberta. We put coffee on to brew, then crossed the street to a convenience store that featured some bakery goods. The pastries were too sweet, but we knew that my friends Frank and Linda, our next hosts, were preparing healthy salads, free-range chicken, and buffalo, for us that evening, so we would recover.

When we passed the controlled entrance to the Parkway, the spectacular highway that runs south down the spine of the Canadian Rockies past the Columbia Icefields to Lake Louise, we were asked if we were going to Calgary. We were not and were waved through without explanation. As we learned later, the Trans-Canada Highway, heading east towards Calgary, was already closed at Banff. However, our intended route ran north to south through Jasper, Banff and Kootenay National Parks to Radium Hot Springs and, then through the East Kootenay valley to Cranbrook, an incredibly beautiful 500 km drive.

Our first photo stop was at Athabasca Falls. I had stopped here many times, but the site was much improved with walkways that allow visitors very close access to the falls and the gorge below. The water was higher and stronger than I had ever seen before. About 15 km further up the road we stopped at Sunwapta Falls, another tremendous surge of water. When we arrived at the Athabasca Glacier, the tongue of the Columbia Icefields that extended nearly to the highway when I began my first summer job there exactly fifty years before, it was a shockingly tiny remnant of its former self. The historic roadside chalet where I had worked had been replaced by a modern monster lodge. We did not linger long.

When we tried to head south, a truck was parked across the highway. A man spoke to each car in turn. He told us the road ahead had been blocked by two mudslides and he estimated a ten-hour delay, at least. Gundy was not yet aware of how significant a problem we faced.

As we drove the 100 km back to Jasper in increasingly heavy rains, I explained to her the two choices we had. By the shorter route, we would travel in Alberta, northeast past Edson, south through Rocky Mountain House to the David Thompson Highway, east to Red Deer, south through Calgary to Fort MacLeod, and then west through the Crowsnest Pass to

Cranbrook. The other route was in British Columbia, west to Tête Jaune Cache, southwest through Valemount and Clearwater to Kamloops, east past the Shuswap Lakes, through Salmon Arm and past Revelstoke, over the Rogers Pass to Golden, southeast to Radium Hot Springs and then south to Cranbrook. I much preferred the Alberta route as it was just over 900 km in total. Gundy, who disliked Calgary, and knew prairie driving was boring, did not want to go through Alberta. I agreed to go by the much more scenic BC route, realizing that we would not make it to Cranbrook that night. We had no other information to make our decision, but it would prove to be the best decision.

As we neared Mt. Robson again, the rain ceased and the highest mountain in the Canadian Rockies was nearly two thirds visible. We stopped for photos and for the first time learned from other travelers there was extensive flooding happening in Alberta and many roads were closed. I felt much better about Gundy's prescient decision to avoid Alberta.

The day turned sunny as we drove south and followed the glacial North Thompson River on its route to join the Thompson River. Gundy enjoyed the lush, green beauty of a drive she had never before taken. When we stopped in Clearwater some hours later, Gundy encouraged me to continue with our plans to visit Frank and Linda, albeit just for one night instead of two. I agreed and phoned Frank to explain we would not arrive that night but would arrive the next day. He was well aware of the flooding and told us the roads through Kootenay National Park, and through the Crowsnest Pass, had also been closed, but that the route we had chosen was still open.

We stopped briefly in Kamloops at a highway restaurant for a disgusting, over-priced meal. I was worried about Rogers Pass which lay ahead. It is often closed by slides. I knew we needed to get over the pass that night, if it was still open. Golden was still four hours away. By the time we re-fueled in Salmon Arm, the rains had started again. It was pouring and nearly dark as we passed our former home of Revelstoke and began the climb up Rogers Pass. By the summit, our headlights were so ineffective in the blinding rain that I pulled over and attempted to clean them to get a little more illumination. As we started driving again, I said I wished a big truck or something with stronger lights would pass us, so I could follow its tail-lights. A minute later, a gigantic pickup truck overtook us. I did not let it get away until we had reached the flats at the bottom of the east side of the pass.

We checked into a motel in Golden at midnight. I had driven more than 1000 km since breakfast. It was the eve of the longest day of the year (in the Northern Hemisphere), but it felt like we had already had the longest day.

Epilogue

We had 250 km to drive the next morning from Golden to Cranbrook. Just 68 km north of our destination, a massive highway bridge across the Kootenay River at Skookumchuck began to fail and was closed. There were no alternative routes. We had to turn around and retrace our drive 400 km to Revelstoke. We never did get to visit Frank and Linda.

A Trans-Atlantic Flight (in 2016)
by Mary Mae Lewis

The first inkling, on this trip, that all would not be perfect was when we checked our baggage in at Manchester airport. The larger suitcase was opened up before we were allowed through to security and the plane was delayed.

I was by then hungry, and nervous. Boarding in silence the air hostesses only nodded as we took up our seats. There was no welcome aboard and no life jacket demonstrations. Summoning a flight attendant, to obtain earphones, took three attempts. But at four euros a pair we made do with watching an Icelandic film with sub-titles. Only a coffee came, complimentary. Food had to be purchased! With baguettes at eight euros, minimum, we declined (we were used to Spanish prices) *There'll be a hot meal on the six-hour haul from Iceland onwards, surely?*

Arriving at the airport in Reykjavik we felt like we had been disgorged into a refugee camp; bodies sitting on rucksacks littered the transit lounge. Amid the chatter and foul smells, like Hyacinth and Richard in *Keeping Up Appearances* we toured the salon. With my sciatica, sitting on a floor was not a healthy option!

Luckily, hubby spotted an empty seat and nudged me. In a flash I whipped off my sun hat and hurled it, like a Frisbee, across the room. It landed admirably but as I staggered towards it I heard, "Would Mrs Mary Mae Lewis, make her way to the Icelandic Air information desk."

"That's me." I gasped as I handed my husband my bag.

"Mrs Mary Mae Lewis." The voice over the tannoy repeated.

"Guard the seat." I instructed.

"Mrs Lewis?" The girl at the airline counter queried.

"Yes"

"You have been chosen; a random customer."

I moved closer to the pretty face and smiled.

I imagined I had been signalled out for a bottle of free champagne or some luxury chocolates.

"For an extra security check."

Before my chin could drop, I felt an arm on my elbow and I was gently frog marched up some stairs and delivered to the USA BORDER CONTROL.

Passengers lined one wall, holding passports. I wasn't. Showing the US guard my empty hands I was ordered to fetch mine!

I did.

I plead; we only have thirty minutes before boarding. I am frisked and quickly cleared! Phew!

We encamp to the eatery, another queue! *Stuff that.* I grab the only stool available at the bar but with drinks at fifteen dollars a time we order tap water. We talk to an American student about how terrible it would be for America if Donald Trump was elected president and we forget our hunger, till the flight is called.

"I see you have passed your security check," the boarding pass checker announces loudly as we line up, again. I blush and my tummy rumbles like a roller coaster.

"When's dinner?" I enquire as the stewardesses move up and the plane's cabin again like Stepford wives.

"When you order it," one girl says, whipping the menu, (the same one as before) from the pouch on the back of the seat in front of me.

I succumb. Hubby doesn't.

"I'll have the tapas with the wine." Included was a piece of hot pizza, apparently! The wine was fine but the box of tapas, which looked about a foot long on the photo on the menu was no bigger than a big box of matches! The pepperoni looked like burnt spaghetti, the cheese was just one mouthful of cream cheese, and the pizza didn't exist.

"A printing error" the flight attendant informed me. I grimaced and delved into my book, sipped the wine slowly and ignored my hunger pangs.

With face and finger print recognition technology we slipped through Immigration like silver fish through pin holes and waited at the carousel for our suitcases.

Hubby stacked the first one onto his trolley with our hand luggage and coats and we waited and waited. *Damn it our case is lost!* And my hat's in Iceland!

"Ok. No big deal" hubby assures me as he turns to a guard nearby.

"You grab the trolley and we'll do what we have to do."

"Hell, where is the trolley!" I scream as my eyes run around the vicinity looking for our distinctive blue and white suitcase. Spotting a man pushing our stuff down the baggage hall I run up to him.

"What the hell do you think you are doing?" I shout. "You know that trolley isn't yours; those things are not yours. Why did you do this?"

"Cause I am an asshole" he yells. I yank the trolley off him and turn away.

"You said it." I shout, over my shoulder.

"She called me an asshole" the man complained to the guard.

"No, I didn't." I defended myself.

"No, you didn't ma'm. "The man is what he said, an AH but don't worry about that now. You got your stuff back and now you must make a claim for the missing baggage, in the office."

I glance at my watch; we have already missed the 7 pm bus and now will have to wait till 10. Still enough time to get a Big Mac and fries. My mouth waters at the thought.

Mr. Peterson fills out the forms while telling us his life story and we tell him about our son and his family in Milwaukee, who we will be staying with for three weeks; we feel confident our suitcase will turn up. Just one week later it and delivered straight to our son's front door.

We had a lovely holiday in Wisconsin and a good journey home, but I never did see my hat again!

A Weekend on the River
by Robyn Boswell

After 90 days on our Aussie road trip it was time to take a break. By the time we got to Noosa, where we'd been several times before, the thought of camping yet again wasn't particularly enticing so we pitched our tents in a local camping ground with a distinct lack of enthusiasm. As we drove along the banks of the nearby Noosa River a sign caught our attention: 'Houseboat on the River – special weekend rates'. It was Friday, it was meant to be, so in no time at all we'd booked for two nights on the river.

Boarding wasn't before 5pm, so we spent an enjoyable, if somewhat grubby, afternoon digging up thundereggs at a local thunderegg farm. We headed back to camp to pack our gear, while Noel went to make final arrangements for the houseboat. He came racing back to say we weren't able to take it out after sunset and since sunset was at 5.30 and it was already 4.55 a mad panic ensued. I raced into a supermarket to buy groceries feeling like I'd won a grocery grab competition as I frantically filled a trolley.

We zoomed back to camp, grabbed our gear and made it to the boat at 5.25 – phew!

The aptly named 'Gypsy' was like a caravan on a barge. After months of camping; hot and cold running water, a kitchen, shower, TV and radio (that didn't work) and real, albeit very hard beds were five-star luxury to us. It was powered by a 25hp Suzuki outboard, a little less powerful than our boat at home, but very familiar.

We motored a little way off-shore and moored amongst a bevy of other boats for the night. Noel had fun zipping up and down the river in the large plastic dinghy that came with Gypsy. We enjoyed dinner out on deck and played a noisy game for once without having to worry about the sound annoying our neighbours.

The river had the sheen of polished glass in the clear morning light. We ate our breakfast on the aft deck, watching the antics of the local pelicans as they performed their morning ablutions, feeling like we were living a millionaire lifestyle. After breakfast we set off up Noosa River, puttering peacefully along through mangroves and bush. Civilization disappeared rapidly behind us as we were enveloped in the sounds and smells of the cool rainforest. We soon reached Lake Cooroibah, a large lake that averaged only 30cm deep, so keeping to the dredged channel was imperative. Motoring

144

further on up the river, past a few houses and a cable ferry, we reached Lake Coothanabra and anchored off Boreen Point.

A long, sandy beach crowded with picnickers fringed a rustic looking settlement, so Deb, Noel and I set out in the dinghy to explore. Even with the three of us trying our hardest, the extremely heavy dinghy was almost impossible to pull up on the shore. Noel and I grabbed the anchor rope to pull as Deb pushed the stern. Suddenly disaster struck! The anchor rope came adrift and Noel tumbled onto this back and lay there like a stranded beetle, his arms and legs waving in the air. Deb and I collapsed on the sand, laughing until we cried. What unexpected entertainment the other beachgoers had that day!

We discovered a minigolf course that resembled a farmer's untamed cow paddock. Having played every minigolf course we'd come across the length and breadth of Australia, we couldn't give this one a miss. It was arranged in a series of terraces down a hillside, with a hole on each terrace and after climbing to the top, you played your way to the bottom. Deb started at the first hole, gave her ball a generous tap and we watched as it bounced through a fence, over a path, through another fence and scored a perfect hole in one in the last hole. Game over! Our screams of laughter brought people running to see what was going on. And for the record it was the first – and only – time – I won.

Back on board Gypsy, we moseyed down the river and tied up to some trees where we could spend the night. After being on the move for so many weeks, just sitting and being one with the spectacular natural environment that surrounded us was a real morale booster. We snoozed, read and just contemplated life. Noel caught a couple of catfish after a desultory fish and let them go again. At sunset we rowed quietly down the river, stopping to drift and listen to the sounds of the bush around us as we watched and listened to a myriad of birds as they finished their day's activities and settled down for the night. The silence of the night was only broken by the occasional croak of a frog.

After a typical Aussie wake-up call from the cackling kookaburras and vulgar crows, the morning slid peacefully by. We were fascinated by the aptly named whipbirds whose song started with a long, piercing note that rose and rose until it suddenly finished with a crack as loud as a stockman's whip. A couple of whistling kites soared around us diving down and skimming the surface, never missing their targets as they scooped up unfortunate fish. Dad took the dinghy and anchored out in mid-river to spend a couple of quiet hours with his sketchbook.

We were incredibly reluctant to tear ourselves away but eventually pottered unhurriedly back down the river to Noosaville, then sat off-shore, slowly becoming re-accustomed to people and cars and noise.

We had a last few hours of enjoying the sunshine out on deck as we girded our loins for the last section of our wonderful safari – in 13 more days we'd be back in Melbourne's winter, more than 2500 kms away, contemplating a return to the mundane matters of work and 'real life'.

Gypsy

Fair Exchange is No Robbery
by Ronald Mackay

An old maxim says: 'fair exchange is no robbery'. While proverbs sound wise by making bold assertions, we can often poke holes in them.

Just think: 'Absence makes the heart grow fonder'. That so? What about that time we went to summer camp and returned to find our best friend had captured the affections of our sweetheart? Or: 'All good things come to him who waits'. Oh yeah? Do we get an A grade by hanging about or by working hard? Then there's: 'An apple a day keeps the doctor away'. Really? So, farmers with orchards enjoy better health than those who milk cows or grow corn?

I had reason to contemplate the veracity of 'Fair exchange is no robbery' one evening in 1961 at a tiny inn on the road between Burgos and Bilbao.

For several days I'd been hitch-hiking north from the port of Seville on the Guadalquivir in Andalusia. In the Spain of yesteryear, cars were few and far between and tended to be travelling only between this village and the next. Long-distance trucks were the hitch-hiker's salvation.

That evening, a bulk tanker-truck had stopped for me.

"We're transporting wine from Ciudad Real to Bilbao," the taller driver told me.

"In one long haul," boasted the shorter.

I'd hit the jackpot! On Franco's primitive Spanish roads, that meant close to a 24-hour drive with pit-stops. I could sit in comfort in the cab all evening, sleep all night, and be dropped off in Bilbao early next morning. I climbed aboard!

The drivers turned out to be entertaining, happy-go-lucky fellows delighted to be out on the road, happy to be away from home. They were overjoyed to discover that I spoke Spanish. I'd just spent a year working in the banana plantations in Tenerife. Now I was heading back home to Scotland brim-full of travellers' tales.

My surplus of stories contrasted sharply with my lack of money. So, when they stopped for an evening meal at an inn much too expensive for my meagre budget, I opted to sit outside and feast on the aromas.

"Noo! You must eat! You have many days of travel ahead of you to reach Sweden!" said the taller of the two. For Spaniards, the geography of Europe was a mystery.

"I'm not hungry," I lied.

"Hombre, your stomach's been rumbling louder than a diesel engine," said the shorter of the two. "Come! Eat!"

"Our invitation," said the taller. And so, I was persuaded.

It was perhaps 8 o'clock, still early for Spain where dinner begins around 10 p.m. Though the dining room was tastefully decorated, and the tables laid with shining silver and crisp linen napkins, there were no diners at this hour. The innkeeper was surprised to have early guests. He was also a little taken-aback, though he disguised it well, to see two carefree truck drivers and a kilted Scot, stride into his hostelry demanding the menu.

When the confident truckers ordered three portions of roasted goat, roast potatoes, a plate of salad and loaves of bread, his jaw dropped. I'd often dined with the truckers who gave me lifts but it was invariably in small restaurants that served bowls of steaming lentils or perhaps plates of rice topped with fried eggs.

Before we'd wiped our plates clean, the innkeeper placed the bill on the table. He deliberately took up a position between us and the door.

The shorter driver smiled and leaned back in his chair. "We have no money!"

"Not a single peseta!" added his taller partner.

I froze and avoided the innkeeper's eyes.

"You can't pay?" The innkeeper exploded. "You stride into my inn, order my best dishes and then tell me you won't pay?"

Both truckers continued to smile.

"Who said we can't pay?" said the shorter.

"Did we say we won't pay?" asked the taller?

The innkeeper scratched his head. "You want me to call the Guardia Civil?"

I'd had some experience of the Beneméritos, as they were called, and prayed that these rifle and machine gun-toting para-militaries, would not be summoned.

"We said," repeated the shorter driver, "that we have no money."

"However, we fully intend to pay for that delicious meal, and to pay in full," said the taller driver.

"Our truck is outside."

"We're on our way from Ciudad Real to Bilbao."

The innkeeper was catching on. "Ciudad Real? Wine country!"

"Exactly," said the shorter.

"Thirty thousand litres of quality vino tinto," added the taller.

"I'll fetch my empty demijohns," said the innkeeper.

"We have a syphon," offered the short driver.

"You can make up the difference?" asked the tall driver.

"Vinegar!"

"Ideal!"

"These Basques can't tell the difference!"

And so, for the next half hour, the drivers stood atop the tank siphoning quality wine into one demijohn after another. The innkeeper hustled them down into his cellar and swapped them for vinegar.

When the transfer was done, and the tank-caps screwed down tight again, all three looked satisfied.

The innkeeper pumped the hand of each driver. "Fair exchange is no robbery!" He announced the maxim as a moral truth.

"Fair exchange is no robbery!" chorused the two rascals.

Silently, I wondered. Is an exchange fair if the object transferred belongs not to the bestower, but to an oblivious third party? I still hadn't found the answer as I nodded off to sleep.

That's why today, when I hear a credible proverb slip effortlessly off someone's lips, I stop to wonder if it expresses a universal truth or if it might be, on reflection, just a tiny little bit misleading.

Old Hand
by Lu Barnham

Beyond the trickling fountains of the Green Café lies the chaos of Ahmedabad proper, the 16th century Sidi Saiyyed mosque just visible beyond the throng. Famous for its latticework windows, intricately carved with trees and flowers, it's one of the city's most beloved monuments. It's only fifty metres away but traffic in Ahmedabad is a seething, rushing, sprawling organism and I am not looking forward to crossing the road. In fact, I'm stalling. I order a strong cappuccino, in the hope it might give me the energy to make the crossing. The population here is at least 5.5 million and it seems like everyone's on the road today. Some silly part of me thinks I'm going to end up like a smooshed margherita pizza, spread across the paving. But this is my fifth time in India. I should be an old hand by now.

I stand, surveying the relentless traffic. I wait for maybe a minute. In modern life, we're wired to feel like that's an eternity. Traffic is one way but piling in from two different roads, like two separate schools of fish joining in an ocean current. I must watch both to time my move, and yet there *is* no good time to make a move. Spaces exist for a mere second before becoming swallowed again in a spume of autos and cars and bikes. I've learned by now that without a certain bold assertiveness, you can stand by the side of the road in Ahmedabad for the rest of your life. They'll find your skeleton piled there, looking gape-mouthed at the watch dangling off its bony wrist. I've done this countless times, I remind myself. I pick my moment. I pick it wrong.

The stream of traffic closest to me does indeed have a gap. I clear this part nicely and begin to congratulate myself. Unfortunately, the next section is faster than I predicted and includes a bus. An odd rule emerged from my previous experiences of Indian road-crossing; an idea that despite how much it looks like you're destined to become a pancake, things just mould, stretch and bend, and somehow pedestrians make it through unscathed. I'm not so sure this outlook applies this afternoon.

Forced to stand and wait in the middle of the road, with both flows of traffic converging like a *sangam*, I desperately remind myself that this is a country where vehicles, cows and people fight for road space constantly – if the cows can do it, so can I, though I lack the important distinction of being sacred. The bus is problematic. The driver has, fortunately, seen me but the vehicle's great length, relative slowness and the angle as which it takes the corner conceals my appearance from all the impatient vehicles beside and behind it. As each swerves to squeeze past the bus, they're given mere milliseconds to spot the (now somewhat pale) foreigner standing in the middle of the road. I grit my teeth in recognition of my own hopelessness – all I can do is stand here and wait to be hit, because I will, I realise, be hit, by whichever vehicle is the first to have too little time to react.

An autorickshaw swerves at the last minute. Behind it, a man on a white motorbike is coming fast, seeing me too late – I clench my muscles because this is it. He hits the brakes, but we still collide. I feel the force and heat of the rubber on the front tyre slamming my right shin, the wheel still revolving. I can tell the back wheel has left the ground by a foot or so; I feel the weight of the bike change as it presses against my bone. The biker and his vehicle tip a little way upwards then bump and bounce back to the ground. He's still in his seat. I'm still on my feet, though I've been knocked a metre or so back. Time stands absolutely still as we wait, wide-eyed, to see if this is only us, or a pile up. Will the vehicles behind have time to react? Amazingly, they do. They make a path around us on both sides. They flow on, indifferent. The action, briefly plunged in dramatic slow motion, returns to real time; sound, briefly muted, returns. My heart drumming, traffic whirring. The driver and I stare at one another, paralysed by shock. And then he runs his hands through his hair, and hangs his head emotionally, rubbing his forehead, deeply stressed. I'm by his side. He exhales in loud, terrified relief. The colour has drained from his face. My own has returned, a deep, shameful blush. I'm overwhelmed with guilt.

'Are you ok?' I ask, 'I'm so sorry. It's not your fault. You couldn't see me.'

He leans his head against the visor on the front of his bike, breathing deeply, trying to compose himself. Physically, he's fine, but he looks a little like he might cry. I know it would be inappropriate to touch his shoulder, so I pat the front of his bike reassuringly.

'Please don't worry. It's alright.' I can't stand here forever. I begin to look for gaps in the traffic. The biker snaps out of his funk.

'Are *you* ok?' he calls after me.

'I'm fine,' I reassure gently. My impatience put not only myself but others in danger. Every time that poor guy drives around that corner, he's going to get chills, remembering this. I feel like a jerk. I only have one more day left in India – if I concentrate all my energy on not killing myself or anyone else, I might make it to the plane in one piece.

151

I'm dazed as I study the rose-coloured stone of the Sidi Saiyyed mosque, ignoring the increasingly hot throbbing emanating from beneath my right knee.

'Hey, you!' calls a merry autorickshaw driver, as he spots me rounding the corner, 'you should watch where you're going!' No kidding.

Typhoid; or, a prosaic illness in India
by Philip East

'Stop crying!' exclaims the flustered nurse as she drives the needle clumsily into her patient's hand, 'Why are you crying!'

The young barefoot boy in loose-fitting shirt and torn trousers, a hospital porter of sorts, idly scraping the filth from under his fingernails, looks up disinterestedly. The nurse cannot find the vein, yet undeterred she continues to strain, tugging and pulling at the blackening skin. Sobs turn to screams, 'Stop, stop, leave me alone!'

These cries, from my beleaguered girlfriend, Carla, worn out after two weeks of unbroken fever and crippling lethargy, punctuated only by these occasional visits for treatment, are too much. I stagger back as the affronted nurse storms past with her assistant, roused into action at last, in tow, and collapse in a chair. The heat, the screams, it is all too much. The sordid walls smeared by countless dirty hands begin to spin...

The beginning of this tale, the introduction that led to the chaotic scenes described above, is much less dramatic. It begins in Diu, an enclave to the south of Gujarat, in India. A former Portuguese territory, Diu is very much the lesser known cousin of Goa to the south. Yet with a pretty coastline, a mammoth fort, and lots of lovely little Portuguese streets with their stone crosses and Virgin statues that light up at night, it is a peaceful and pleasant setting -- and a rather fitting one for the onset of typhoid. For it is in Diu that Carla's symptoms developed; as gentle sea breezes blew through the whitewashed streets, the *Salmonella* Typhi bacteria multiplied. Nothing explosive, just the calm and gradual increase of fever.

With hindsight, I somehow thought typhoid would be more exotic and terrible. In the West, with our injections and our tablets and our sterile environments, we only have an exposure to serious communicable diseases through history and the media. Epidemics 'rage' and people are infected by the thousands, all sallow-faced and poverty-stricken. Yet Carla seemed alright really, the same pretty girl whom I love; perhaps a little tired and worried, after all, a prolonged high fever is never a good sign, but not on her deathbed by any means, especially in such a tranquil setting. Yet sickness became routine, a routine of simmering fear and constant wistfulness, from which the only relief was the hospital.

Though new, the hospital at Diu contains in microcosm all the dogmas and chaos that India is built upon. A small hillock of beaten sandals adorns the entrance, each patient diligent in their removal as they would at the temple or mosque. Moving further in, beyond the occasionally staffed desk, a long corridor of shaky metal seats acts as a disorganised waiting room of sorts. There is no order here, a doctor is prescribed, but when they see you, if they will see you, is left open, just like the doors. People barge in and wander out at leisure, as ladies in blue-pop and cherryade pink saris wander by with sloshing mop buckets. When at last a doctor is procured the diagnosis is never the same. Sometimes typhoid, sometimes not. More blood tests. More urine samples. More confusion. The attempt at intravenous antibiotics on the third visit was the last straw however, it was time to leave.

We could have gone to Mumbai, with its superior healthcare and stifling May humidity -- a tropical jungle of concrete where everything has a price: and quality is certainly not guaranteed. But the heat and risk, after weeks of fever already, seemed too much. Instead, it was back to the sterility of Europe, cleanliness being a blessing when the fragility of human life becomes so apparent. Of course, it seems selfish to have the option to run away, but the sense of relief was palpable, the shedding of a heavy burden. Escape yielded results as well, a stringent series of tests and a strong course of antibiotics were all it took, and just as it started, typhoid slowly faded away.

Despite what happened my memories of Diu are fond, if somewhat vivid. I can still see the giant leathery bats surging from the forest at dusk, wave after wave of squealing dark forms swooping low over the rooftops; or, meandering by the great Portuguese fort, the surf fizzing and crashing into the bastions below, gentle herders in their bright red turbans, grizzled by the sun, stop to chat amid the arid scrub and tinkling of bells. Scenes of utter melancholy, a fitting word, perhaps, for typhoid.

Now, with two years already past, people still recoil and seemed shocked that we left India because of typhoid. It appears so extreme, so dangerous, so exotic? And although it is true that sanitation and healthcare are indeed appalling in India, shocking even, it is also true that these diseases we fear so much from afar are ever so prosaic and commonplace in reality. The day before we left Diu I wandered from our guesthouse to a small restaurant where I often took breakfast. Already dripping in sweat after a brisk walk in the fierce, grey Indian sunshine of Summer, I chatted with the waiter. Mentioning the possibility that Carla had typhoid he recoiled in shock. And yet, when I, taken aback inquired, 'But is it rare to contract typhoid here in India?'

He retorted, 'Oh, no, I have had it twice!'

Diu

Conrad Maldives Rangali Island
by Colleen MacMahon

The sea, like the past, is another country; I feel things differently there.

At night the Indian Ocean has a particular magic, its moon drenched surface glistening and shifting seductively as I walk across the deck of the water villa to the wooden steps. It is some time after midnight and the island is quiet, apart from the rustle of fruit bats as they settle in the trees, and the gentle slap of the water against the shore. The other villas have been folded into the darkness, their occupants apparently already asleep or just not tempted, as I am, to swim naked with the sharks.

In January the air temperature here is as warm in the wee small hours as human breath and the water is like silk. Public nudity is forbidden in the Maldives, a rule necessarily to be respected and observed during daylight hours; but the seclusion of a private villa on this, the smaller and arguably more exclusive of the two islands which make up this resort, allows total privacy and freedom at night. It is both exhilarating and unnerving. I slip into the water, seduced by its sensuous caress and thrilled by my aloneness. There really are sharks (some of them at least two feet long) swimming within inches of me, illuminated by the contained light from a small lamp on the deck. Unfazed by my presence they glide around my legs, accompanied by a corps de ballet of curious fish. Whatever the black tipped reef sharks are hunting in these shallow waters it is not me, or even their immediate companions; there is a calm and enchanting beauty about this scene, and the fish nibbling at my toes and fingers are amusing as they dart in and away again for each quick kiss. But further out in the darkness, where the waters are deep and enthrallingly mysterious, I know there is real danger.

Beyond the natural perils of the oceans there are other threats. Somewhere, perhaps not very far from here as the fruit bat flies, there is another island. It is higher above sea level than the lush, talcum sanded resorts where we tourists stay and therefore – ironically - may survive the rising tides around it for longer. It was made by us, out of our rubbish, and is a silent reminder of the cost of privilege and pleasure.

I may never again be able to afford to come here, or perhaps by the time I can there will be no sands left in which to leave a footprint – carbon or otherwise. I don't know how to reconcile my love of travel with the damage I may do in the process, or how to balance my assumed right to discover and explore with my responsibility to preserve and protect. If we push Nature too far she will need to push back, or perhaps we will engineer our own downfall before it is entirely too late...

For this magical moment though, whilst I swim in the spangled darkness with my sharks, I am in paradise and entirely content.

La Camioneta de Cerveza
by Amy L. Bovaird

Renata and I struck up an unlikely friendship. We couldn't have been more different. Like most Colombian city girls, she looked like she stepped off the pages of *Glamour*. With her immaculate make-up—from well-penciled eyebrows to highly-contoured cheeks and deep red lips—she intimidated me.

Both in our mid-twenties and from the same church, once in a while we took in a movie or sipped thick, pulpy juices, but we had never traveled out of town together. This time she invited me to meet her family in Corro Morro.

I threw on a pair of blue jeans and t-shirt with sneakers, and, traveled light with an old army backpack. Renata wore a tanktop, short-sleeved tailored jacket, and pressed blue jeans. She carried a red valise in her hand and looked even taller in her three-inch heels.

Though I was as casual as Renata was chic, I still held clout as a foreigner. This status, I suspected, brought about the invitation.

On the bus, Renata leaned over and said, "Amy, I translate. No worries."

"I can speak Spanish," I assured her, knowing my foreign language skills far surpassed her belabored attempts at conversation in fragmented English. Like most locals, she wanted to practice English, so I deferred to her.

The bus came to a shuddering halt when it reached Corro Morro. As is typical in Latin American *pueblitos*, whole families congregated around the market square--a large central fountain, flower-lined walkways, a park and a church, all situated together. The crumbling, solid-colored but faded, painted buildings were lettered in black--*Supermercado, Restaurante, Gasolinera.*

The locals slowed or stopped all together to stare at me, the *gringa*. Renata reigned in her glory and introduced me as a "close" friend. When people tried to strike up conversations with me, however, she cut them off. "*Ella no habla español.*"

She *knew* I spoke Spanish. I gritted my teeth and bore the lie, so she would appear more cosmopolitan.

Renata's father, a pharmacist, held status in Corro Morro. Although he was considered wealthy there, her family lived extremely humbly by American standards. In fact, my guest bed was a door perched on top of two sawhorses with a sheet spread over the wood, no mattress and a light cover for me to use. I can't remember how my makeshift "bed" didn't tip over, but their ingenuity intrigued me.

The visit itself was unremarkable until it came time to leave. A monsoon-like rainstorm struck the night before and washed out the roads. All public transportation stopped, and we were stranded.

I needed to return to Bucaramanga in Santander, another state, to teach the following day. We started hitchhiking, with no luck, slip-sliding through the streets. Mud covered our clothing—more mine than Renata's. I even had splatters of mud in my hair.

When we reached the outskirts of town, Renata stopped. "Time to eat."

"But what about Bucaramanga?" I asked, fearing a long delay. I imagined arriving home in the wee hours, the Mud Monster Incarnate.

"We'll find a ride," Renata promised.

A short, heavy-set older woman served as the waitress in this hole-in-the-wall joint. She smiled shyly at me, showing off her only tooth and took our order. I asked for *pollo asado*, grilled chicken.

The waitress nodded and scrawled it down. "Jorgé," she called, pointing to a scrawny chicken in the side yard. A teenage boy caught it, and ignoring the squawking, wrung its neck. I sat in shocked silence, unable to look away. It was that poor chicken that caused me to be a vegetarian for the next year and a half.

As we waited, Renata ducked in and out of her seat. "*We have a ride,*" She pumped her arm. "*Viajamos en una camionetta de cerveza.*" Of all things, we would travel to Bucaramanga … in a beer truck.

A beer truck? How would a truck make it over washed out and muddy roads that much larger buses wouldn't take on?

As we prepared to leave, Renata pointed to the inside of a brightly-colored truck. I peered in and found the truck jam-packed with crates of filled bottles.

She said, "You can lay down on them. I'll ride in the cab."

Huh?

I *was* the smaller one, so I crawled inside, noting crate upon crate of beer, stacked three levels high. When I lay down on the open-topped boxes, I had only half a foot between me and the truck's canvas ceiling.

"Adios," Renata waved as she backed away and situated herself in the passenger seat of the cab.

After the door closed, I didn't worry about the tight fit because I had to find the handle of the nearest beer crate to keep from sliding or banging my head.

The rickety truck bounced and jounced along the deeply-rutted dirt road, and I bumped and thumped along with it. The tops of the bottles dug into my skin through my clothing, especially when we rounded the curves. The stench of so much beer overwhelmed me.

We stopped shortly after we started our journey. I then learned what motivated the gregarious driver—a strong following and *muchos pesitos*—*lots of money.*

After I discovered what a daring ride I took on, I cushioned my blows with the clothing I took from my backpack. Then I settled in for the many stops I would encounter for the next six hours to Bucaramanga.

Somewhere along that horribly rutted journey, I decided Spanish would become my preferred language for travel, especially with Renata.

One *viaje por camioneta de cerveza* was enough for me.

If I had to have such adventures, at least I would have some bargaining power to tip things my way—in the best-case scenario I'd be drinking the beer instead of riding on top of it!

The translation of *viaje por camioneta de cerveza* is 'journey by beer truck'

Sunday Sevilla
by Alan Passey

5am Sunday. A rooster opens up a conversation with a braying donkey somewhere on the hillside and they're not shy about sharing their opinions. I mentally pushed "snooze" and rolled over. I planned to be up early for the longest ride of the trip so far - 70 miles. There was a sharp chill in the mountain air as I stepped out into the Algodonales morning. Sevilla sits in a geographical basin in the valley of the Guadalquivir River and benefits from a subtropical climate. In simple terms, it was going to get much hotter as the day wore on and so I intended to pace myself and resolved to stop at each petrol station to buy cold water. Regular drinking would be critical to stay hydrated. My prep notes told me that I should check that I have everything I need at El Coronil, since after that point there are long stretches of 'notmuchness' in terms of fuelling stops for at least 30 miles or so.

As the sun rose into the day, I eased along through waving masses of golden wheat fields and sunflowers breaking out their yellow fanned faces towards the sky leading me down to the delightful little town of El Coronil, a short hop off the main road at the end of an avenue of palm trees. Cars whip by the main junction, heading for Ronda or Sevilla, not realising that down the hill is a little gem with a plaza just made for the Sunday papers, a coffee and conversation. Prayers said for the day, the gentry find a shady spot in the square to trade stories and diagnose creaking ailments. Bars are starting to open when I arrive. People hail their friends for intense exchanges as if they haven't seen them for years.

I sipped coke, ate honey and tostados, and wiped dead flies from my shins, content as a group of mountain bikers came through on their club ride.

Back on the road in the hair dryer breeze, by 1.30 I had about 12 miles to go.

I messaged my hostess from a petrol station (cold water refill) to say that I would be early. No problem. I was whipping along. Oh, how pride comes before a fall.

My plan was to enter Sevilla by a route that would take me directly to my apartment and by some fortitude the slip road from the service station took me straight to the junction that I needed. I couldn't believe my luck. However, Mr.Garmin and I had an exchange of words. He kept telling me to u-turn and after a couple of these false starts I realised that I was going around in circles. But I was only 5 miles from Sevilla. What could go wrong?

To cycle into Sevilla, you need to have your route planned meticulously, it seems. Take this from someone who has now experienced it. Cycles are banned from the major A roads into the city even though you've been on the same road for the last 50 miles.

So it was that I found myself at a roundabout facing A roads to Malaga, Jerez and Sevilla and the only other option, somewhere called "San Pedro", notified by a rough, hand painted sign. "San Pedro" it is then.

I began to feel a little uneasy as I bounced along a moon-cratered dirt track between slatted sheds and corrugated shacks, junked cars, machinery and broken glass. I could hear raucous voices and laughter from the 'chabolistas' shanty-town dwellers, but saw no-one, and I hoped that I wasn't going to attract any attention. I felt that this was probably the last place I should be right now. A guard dog thought that I was sport and gave chase, yapping alarm until I managed to outrun him. What am I doing here?

I stumbled out onto a minor road unscathed and thankful, but my bike was limping. Impossible to dodge everything as fast as I could, I'd whacked the rim of a pothole resulting in a hole in my tyre.

By now it was 35 degrees and I'm by the roadside repairing my tyre, getting hotter, hungry and tired. I needed to drink, but my water tasted like I'd done my washing in it. During the next 20 minutes I was passed by half a dozen different vehicles of some sort. One asked if I would like a lift in his truck, with the bike in the back, and 3 more stopped to see if I was okay. I remembered a conversation with my Spanish friend before I left home. I'd said I was worried about mechanical failures on the road. "Don't worry," she said, "there'll always be someone to help you." And so it seemed.

Sunday siesta Sevilla. Six lane highways and hardly a car in sight. It had taken me two and half hours to work out the last 12 miles. My hostess greeted me with a smile and handshake. She didn't seem to mind my oily fingers. She was a cyclist too and we joked about punctures - usually the back wheel - the dirty one. She poured me ice cold water from the fridge and I drank like a man who'd just crawled through a desert. It had indeed been a long hot ride. I was in Sevilla at last. I just love siestas.

Sevilla Street

The Best Little Bank in the World
by Helen Bing

Money. Currencies. How much, how little. Where to go to get more money when the funds are running low. Our bank at home had recommended taking cash with us rather than using cards, because many of the ports we were going to would not necessarily have handy cash machines. We have also always found it nice and easy to have cash to use in market places, where we tourists often congregate. But, we really needed some more American dollars. We had left home with what we thought was enough, but somehow, they were disappearing at an alarming rate.

At home it's straight forward. Go to your bank or a Foreign Exchange, hand over one lot of money get it swapped to another. For a small transaction fee, it's all done.

We assumed it would be the same in America. After all, it was their currency we wanted. Easy, yes? No. Into a very pleasant bank in New London, Connecticut we went. The air outside was steamy hot - the bank was cool. Did they do Foreign Exchange? No, said the lovely staff. Actually, they were seriously lovely, even offering to let my husband and his walker stay there to keep cool while I went to find the other bank. Just go back on to the main road, they said, and take the next road on the right. They'll be able to help you.

Off we went to find a rather imposing building with glass doors and air-conditioned coolness. Bliss. We stood for a moment not sure where to go when a "Can I help?" called to us from behind a bullet proof, glass shielded counter to our left.

"We need to buy some dollars," we say.

"You don't have an account with us, do you. If you want us to help, that will be US$20. Then there's the transaction fees, etc etc."

"Oh," we say. "Thanks for your help anyway. Good bye."

Obviously American banks were not going to be very much use.

And so we continued our travels watching our dollars carefully, which probably wasn't a bad thing, until we got to American Samoa. There, in the centre of town was the ANZ bank, so, not feeling overly hopeful, in I went leaving my husband outside under a shady tree.

Inside there was a large airy room. No fancy air conditioning, just big ceiling fans. And signs to show you where to go.

I went over to the information desk to ask about exchanging some Australian currency (yes I know, I'm a Kiwi not Australian, but that's what the ship works on) to American dollars. It was absolutely possible, no problem at all. After a brief conversation asking me where I was from and being told where her relations were playing rugby, I was given a number and asked to go and sit on one of the chairs that had been placed under the fans. Not a queue in sight. How civilised.

Now the islands are not known for speed, but who cares. I didn't have to stand in a queue, I was cool, and so far, things were going just fine. It took a little while for my number to be called, but finally I went up to the allotted counter. No fancy security here, just a face to face talk with a lovely young teller who, it turned out, had family in Auckland. Fortunately, I had my driver's license on me because I did need a photo ID. No, I hear you thinking, I didn't think to take my passport ashore. My license and my details disappeared into an office somewhere to be photocopied, bits of paper were stamped, drawers were delved into and my lovely bright Aussie dollars were replaced with the somewhat uninspiring, but very useful American equivalent.

Forty-five minutes later I emerged from the bank into the sun of beautiful Pago Pago to find my husband still sitting under the same tree where I had left him. His first thoughts - that bar up the road everybody was saying is so nice.

I left him there with his cool glass of Vailima beer while I went shopping. I really should have got a few more dollars!

The Cape St Vincent (Portugal)
by Angie Clifford

'Petra,' I exclaimed, my eyes nearly popping out of their sockets! 'What are you doing here?'

'Angie,' Petra was all smiles as she embraced me in a warm hug. 'Can't believe I'm here either,' she said, 'spur of the moment, completely un-planned,' she informed me. 'John died two weeks ago, (John, I knew was a long-time friend) and poor Betty (his wife, now widow) was so beside herself with grief, and insisted she pay all my travel and taxis if I would stay with her for a couple of weeks.' Petra continued; I knew Petra in normal circumstances hardly ever travelled, living as she did practically hand to mouth on a UK government pension.

Half an hour ago I had been waiting for the 12.10 from Portsmouth to Waterloo and wondering how I could while away the next few hours. The moon can sometimes appear in the sky during the daytime because it is the closet to earth, and because its orbital cycle means that sometimes it is brighter in the day than at night, this was such a day. As I gazed up into the sky I felt transported into another dimension, time stood still. and into my mind floated a string of words..."Red Moon Rising".

Why are trains never on time, I thought, my frustration levels rising ever so slightly, but finally the 12.10 arrived ten minutes late. I stood patiently as the double doors made that pling pling sound and swung outwards letting off a gaggle of uniformed school kids, followed by a frazzled looking teacher, (all probably heading for the steam engine museum I thought silently). I was just about to board when I felt a hand on my shoulder.

'Excuse me madam,' said a black leather clad biker, 'I think you've dropped this,' he said, handing me a paperback book, before I could protest he had disappeared in the throng. I found myself a seat with a table and made sure I was sitting in a forward-facing position. Placing my luggage in the overhead rack I popped the book down on the table, it was face up now and I could see the title, "Red Moon Rising" I could feel the hairs on the back of my neck stand to attention.

So, now I was a little more than intrigued. I looked at the cover; it was pillar box red with a silhouette of the moon. The author's names Pete Grieg and Dave Roberts were prominent in yellow, below read, Redmoonchronicles#1 The Story of the 24-7 Prayer. I started to read, this book had my attention from the beginning. I had just reached a paragraph that said – "The 24/7 prayer movement started in *Guildford*," when I looked out of the window...I was at *Guildford Station.* Quickly grabbing my luggage from the overhead and clutching the book in the other I got off the train. I was due to catch the Gatwick express, where I would later be flying with Easy Jet to Spain where I lived. And that was where I saw Petra... on Guildford station.

Petra and I were part of a small group of women in Spain. We met once a week to pray for our friends and families, and our communities. We had a passion to help others, and to see miracles. So! This situation suddenly felt a little surreal, I had met one of my prayer partners from Spain, in Guildford, where I had just read a sentence (from a book given to me by a *stranger)* *telling me that a prayer movement (I had never heard of) began its life there... in Guildford!*

Petra and I finally went our separate ways as I boarded the Gatwick Express, and she the Portsmouth bound train. Once my luggage was safely stored in the overhead I continued to read; fascinating, I devoured every word. Peter Grieg it seemed was a man on a mission; by the time I landed at Malaga airport I had finished reading his book.

I felt a huge bubble of excitement rising up from somewhere deep within me as I stepped onto Spanish soil. Pete's book had inspired me. I had read how he had experienced a vision on the Cape St Vincent Portugal where he felt called to start that 24/7 prayer movement. I too loved a little adventure, the unexpected, travel and excitement I felt fully charged and ready to go...to Portugal, and the CAPE.

'Ange,' Jerry said picking up my luggage, 'I've had to park in the Galleries, sorry! Hope you're wearing sensible shoes?' The Galleries' was a last resort car park and a longish walk away, I stifled a grimace, but it would take more than that to burst my joyful bubble, I was ready to "rock and roll".

Two days later, and with the sat nav primed we were on our way. And five hours and two stops later we arrived, in Lisbon Portugal. The budget hotel was perfection; double bed, an en-suite, balcony and charming decor, plus wi-fi (a must these days), thank-you "Booking.Com".

Our visit the next day to the Cape St Vincent was perfect; and was everything I had expected. Wild, rugged and exquisitely beautiful, warm winds caressed us as we explored. The once beautiful wild spring flowers now stood tall, dried out by the intense weeks of summer sun, dead, but speaking far more than words ever could. Yes, I had a mystical experience there. Death waited in the months ahead, and heartache would follow; but I felt a strange peace surround me, death could be beautiful, I had seen that in the flowers.

The Road Home
by Syd Blackwell

The road home can take some unusual turns. Our return from a visit to world-class Iguazu Falls had twists that seemed miraculous.

We arrived in Foz do Iguaçu, the Brazilian city adjacent to the falls, on Thursday evening. During the Friday group visit to the Argentinian side of the falls, our guide informed us that our airline, Pluna, had cancelled the return flight to Montevideo scheduled for Sunday night. He said arrangements with other carriers would be made and he would keep us informed.

By the Saturday tour on the Brazilian side of the falls, most had learned how they would be travelling. We had not. At our hotel, late Saturday afternoon, we received a phone call from a Sao Paulo-based tour representative. The connection was bad; the representative only spoke Portuguese. Neither of us speak Portuguese. We understood someone would phone again Sunday morning. We checked emails hoping that Geant Travel in Montevideo, where we booked this tour, had sent a message. They had not.

On Saturday evening, our group enjoyed a dinner and Brazilian revue. Everyone else knew how they would go home. One young woman, who would be leaving at 6am via Sao Paulo to Montevideo, was a vacationing Pluna employee. Incredibly, when we returned to the hotel after midnight, she gave up some of her valuable sleep time and called Pluna. She got us a confirmed booking on the next Pluna flight leaving Foz do Iguaçu. Unfortunately, not until Tuesday evening. We would never have been able to do this ourselves. We were very grateful.

It appeared we would have to stay two extra days and we had not prepared for this. We went to bed hoping the promised call on Sunday might provide a better answer, but at least we had a way home.

The call finally came at 2:30pm. Again, the agent spoke only Portuguese. The only part of the message Gundy understood was something about 42 kilometres. After repeatedly telling the representative, in Spanish, that she could not understand, he hung up.

We decided to go for a walk. In the lobby, we noticed Darcio, the only English-speaking desk person, was at work. We told him about the call in Portuguese and the poor connection. We asked him to take a message if an agent called back. He decided to call the agent.

He learned we were booked on a flight leaving from Puerto Iguazú, across the Argentinian border, 42 kilometres away. And, we had little more than an hour to get there. But how?

A driver who had arrived to pick up somebody else, overheard the situation. He immediately used his cellphone to call for assistance. He told us a driver named Judo would arrive in about ten minutes and would get us to the airport. How incredibly fortunate he came at just the right moment, overheard the problem, and cared enough to solve it. We hastened to our room to pack.

Judo had his own miracles to work, circumventing a long line-up at the Brazilian border crossing, getting VIP service from the officer at the Argentinian border station, and getting a friendly wave-through from a team of police searchers who were stopping most other vehicles. He spoke English and we had a great conversation. We got to the airport with time to spare. We thanked Judo and said goodbye.

We hurried inside and went to the Argentinian Airlines desk. We had no tickets and no information at all about the flight except the departure time. The agent had three flights leaving that evening. All were fully booked. None matched the departure time we had been given. A computer check, using our passports, revealed we were not booked on any of his flights. He pointed us to LAN, the only other airline desk at this airport. There was a very long line.

As we joined the line, the Argentinian Airline agent reappeared beside us and took us past the whole line to a LAN agent off to one side. We gave him our passports and he quickly confirmed we were booked on this flight and should immediately go back into the line-up. How incredibly thoughtful of that Argentinian Airlines agent to continue to take care of us. We also saw Judo, our driver, still hanging around. He wanted to make sure we were actually going to fly, and, if not, he would take us back to Brazil. Again, incredibly thoughtful.

Soon, the line-up was processed, and very soon after we boarded a LAN plane. Our boarding passes showed we were flying to Buenos Aires. We had no information about what would happen there. Still, it felt good we had got this far so quickly.

In Buenos Aires, we hurried to the LAN desk and were directed to the Pluna desk at the other end of the airport. Again, our passports were enough to get us a boarding pass on a Pluna flight to Montevideo. We had to be at the gate, at the other end of the airport and upstairs, in five minutes. After what we had been through in the last few hours, that was easy.

Through security, we found a couple from Spain who had been part of our tour group. They had also flown from Puerto Iguazú, but on an earlier flight, and would take the same Pluna flight as us to Montevideo. There, they had a rental car waiting to drive to Punta del Este. They offered to take us to our home in Villa Argentina on the way. This last flight was delayed, and we arrived in Uruguay at 10:30pm. The buses that service the airport on Sunday nights are infrequent. However, we no longer needed to wait for one. Incredible!

We were dropped off on the side of the highway adjacent to our home shortly after 11pm. We never imagined such a result as we sat frustrated in our Brazilian hotel room earlier that afternoon, but the universe was looking after us.

Iguazu Falls

Panda Eyes
by Robyn Boswell

From the friend who, in San Francisco, didn't want to ride the cable cars or go to Fisherman's Wharf, to the one who's terrified of escalators, I've found that travelling with friends can be fraught with difficulties.

Shelley and I hadn't known each other long when we shared a hotel room in Los Angeles for a few days. Shelley likes to plan ahead and be in control, whilst I'm more of a 'what will we do now....what's down that road?' traveller. Having made a number of trips by myself, I was happy for her to take charge, so she spent the first evening poring over city maps and local bus timetables as she planned our days.

The first day was the Holocaust Museum. Having been to Dachau, I wasn't convinced, but finding our way there through Beverly Hills on a local bus sounded like an adventure. We got ourselves organised for the day and sat on our beds chatting and taking our morning medications.

Suddenly Shelley glanced at me with a look of horror, clutching a small white pill bottle.

"Oh no. I've taken the wrong pills – I've just taken two sleeping tablets!"

She rushed to the bathroom to try and dislodge them, but it was too late. Thank goodness she'd discovered it before we set out for the day.

We quickly formulated plan B and ordered room service breakfast. Shelley figured that if I came back around 3 pm she might be ready to surface.

As we ate our bacon and eggs, I noticed that Shelley's eating was getting slower and slower. Suddenly she missed her mouth altogether, the forkful of eggs tumbling down the front of her clean shirt. Before I could react, she was sound asleep, clutching another forkful of food neatly poised between her plate and her mouth. I disentangled her from her tray, pulled the covers over her and left her to it.

Unfortunately, the hotel neighbourhood wasn't conducive to foot exploration. The park across the road looked very pleasant, but the cars I had seen pulling up there at all hours of the day and night didn't fill me with enthusiasm to take a walk. There wasn't much else around the neighbourhood and none of it felt particularly safe or interesting. I didn't want to stray too far from the hotel until Shelley woke up.

The only shop nearby was a supermarket. It's amazing how much time you can spend cruising the shelves of a supermarket full of unfamiliar products when you have more time than you need on your hands. It was like a museum of modernity. I read labels, perused products I had never seen before and bought a rather ghastly striped mixture of jam and peanut butter to squeeze into my suitcase. That filled an hour or so....there was still a lot of day to go.

At least the hotel had a pool. It was early in the season and no one was foolish enough to try it but me. It was chilly but I persuaded myself to do a few laps and pretend I was in a tropical paradise..... one more hour gone.

Unfortunately, I'd finished reading the one book I had as I intended to buy one at the airport for my flight. Back in the supermarket I managed to find a not particularly entertaining magazine that was about the lives of people I didn't recognise......one more hour....

At the café next to the hotel I managed to linger over my lunch.......another hour......

Eventually the clock dragged its hands reluctantly around to 3pm and I went to our room and found Shelley trying desperately to shake herself awake. She woke up enough to drag herself to the mirror and burst into gales of laughter. The black circles under her eyes gave her the guise of a half-awake panda!

She was worried that she had wasted one of our days together and wanted to make amends, so suggested we take a taxi to Santa Monica a little way away. Walking down Third Street Promenade I felt like I was accompanied by a zombie. Shelley stumbled along, to all intents and purposes sleepwalking. I enjoyed poking around in the shops and watching the passing parade, which is always entertaining along the promenade. Shelley finally headed for the nearest seat and snoozed until I came back and moved her on to the next one.

Eventually we decided an early dinner and a taxi back to the hotel was necessary, so we sat outside in the sunshine at a pleasant little Italian restaurant and I, at least, enjoyed the flavoursome, aromatic meal. Shelley tried her best to enjoy it with little success. She kept getting slightly strange looks from the wait staff and passing pedestrians. I realised later they were probably used to seeing people who had ingested various substances, but probably not a somewhat conservative, middle-aged lady!

The next day we made it to the Holocaust Museum. The local bus was fascinating and took us through streets we would never have visited on a tour. The museum? Well, we stayed ten minutes – it wasn't what we wanted to do on a fun holiday, that's for sure. The problem was that Shelley with all her organisation had planned for us to take a bus back much later in the afternoon and hadn't considered any contingency plans. We had no idea how to call for a taxi – in my experience that's something that people in Los Angeles can't help you with. Luckily as we sat and contemplated our fate a taxi pulled into a restaurant up the road. I've never seen Shelley move as fast as she did then! It was a very expensive ride back to our hotel after a day of nothing, really.

Fortunately, our last day at my favourite Los Angeles destination, the Getty Centre, made up for everything.

Shelley and I became good friends. We share a sense of humour and have told our story many times over the years.

Stubborn to a Point
by Andrew Klein

I have spent many years out on the road. Often times I found myself, for several reasons, playing music in the crowded streets of places like Oslo, Amsterdam, and London. My voice, accompanied by my guitar, would sing popular folk-rock tunes in exchange for money, refreshments, and even smiles. I always enjoyed these mini concerts and, for the most part, believe the folks passing by felt somewhat the same.

Occasionally my musical sojourns would attract those who would ask me to stop, or move along, or go home. Rather than incur certain troubles I would usually nod, smile, and follow directions. However, there was one occasion with which I refused, and, for some reason stood my ground with fearless, and unshakable petulance.

On the streets of Tokyo those who are doing business must take care not to cross the dreaded Yakuza. If one is making money, but not paying off the Boys then one could find themselves in a world of hurt. The Japanese syndicate would just as soon wipe offenders off the face of the earth as they would collect their 'taxes'. It is in this grey world of street culture that I found myself up against these thugs with only a strong sense of pride, very little linguistic skills, and a strange 'western' idea that injustice cannot carry the day.

I had seen other 'buskers' on a certain corner of the city and knew that, at least most times, it was allowed. In fact, I myself had been there just one day before. However, as luck would have it, this day would be different. There were three of them brandishing the typical attributes of the gang. They each had various lengths of unnaturally curly hair, several visible tattoos, and missing pinky fingers. I really didn't think they looked very scary.

I had just finished a Simon and Garfunkel song when the three came across the road and asked me to move. I knew the Japanese liked the duo's music, so it could not have been the tune I played, but these guys were serious, so I collected a few bills and moved down the street. I Played a Bob Dylan song followed by a Lloyd Cole tune and sure enough, right as I was receiving lots of yen, the boys showed up again and pointed towards the subway and, with raised voices, asked me to get lost.

At this point I said something back to them, which one of them, who I'll call 'Curly', did not like. He kicked my guitar case into the street. I said, "OK, OK I'll leave", and packed up. As I headed towards the trains, I heard another busker playing and I sat down to watch. The boys came around the corner and rather than stop the guy from playing they actually tipped him and kept walking. After a few more tunes he packed up and left. I took the opportunity to play a few more songs in what I felt was a safe spot. A Neil Young tune followed by a Beatles number and then the Boys showed up again. They seemed upset. Curly was yelling about something, and I reminded them that the other foreigner played right before me. I could not understand what their problem was.

Curly cursed me and then came at me with a knife drawn. I put my hands up and said, "OK, OK, I'll go", but Curly had enough of me and poked at me with the blade while cursing loudly. The other two stopped him from killing me and he was so upset at his loss of face that he swung and clipped me in the cheek. At that moment another gang member came and yelled at Curly. He turned to me and explained, in English, that I must not make that guy upset as he is crazy. He said I could play one more song and then never return to that street again. I thanked him and sat down to play a beautiful rendition of 'Tangled up in Blue' by Bob Dylan. I collected a fair bit of yen for that one and then packed up and headed for the train back to my place. As I walked along, I said to whoever was listening, 'I really didn't think I was that bad'.

Ellan Vannin
by Susan Mellsopp

Swaying from side to side the huge catamaran roared and shuddered as it was hit by enormous waves. Rearing up then dropping violently into the trough the Seacat then rose out of the Irish Sea and slammed from side to side into the grey swirling water. Silence reigned momentarily as all I could hear was the throbbing of the engines. Then the thunderous roar filled my ears again as the hull rose to meet the groaning sea and spray rained down on all sides. I wondered how long I would survive if the hull snapped and we were thrown into the water.

Not one to get seasick, or scared by a briny adventure, I was thoroughly enjoying this ferry ride from Port Douglas in the Isle of Man to Liverpool. Nibbling on a packet of chips and devouring nuts I had stored in my backpack after arriving in London 6 weeks earlier, I watched with amusement as white-faced passengers and terrified children clung to seats and rails, often sliding across the floor as they attempted to change seat or run for the toilets. Visibility was nil, but we had been informed that the captain was taking a direct route to the English coast. He would then travel down to Liverpool in the lee of the land hoping to avoid the worst of the lashings of this force nine gale.

My neighbour is Manx, and her cousin had kindly invited me to stay on my trip to the island, quite unusual for the reserved and very private locals. I had travelled over on a glassy soft blue sea from Heysham, dozing after a frantic day which began in Manchester. The house I had stayed in was filthy dirty and smelt foul; I had feared for my health. Waking suddenly when accosted by a group of rugby mad Irishmen who had noticed my Kiwi lapel badge; they were ecstatic to discover I came from Chiefs country, our local rugby team. Their joy turned to abject disappointment when I explained I was probably the one New Zealander they would ever meet who hated rugby.

When the ferry docked, I discovered I was expected to be a guest in an hour's time at the Women's Institute meeting in Ramsey. Visions of the Calendar Girls and Jerusalem swam before my eyes. Grubby and very hungry, all I had eaten that day was a sandwich snatched between train journeys, I felt uncomfortable. The reticent nature of the Manx was disconcerting, I was an intruder. I had met some of them when they had visited New Zealand, but they failed to acknowledge me. The speaker was enthralling. Almost seven feet tall and weighing about twenty stone, the drum major from the local pipe band regaled us with stories about his uniform and role in various island ceremonies. This included the opening of the Manx parliament at Tynewald. My audibly rumbling tummy was soon calmed with a huge slice of cream filled Victoria sponge, chocolate eclairs and Eccles cakes. I never did get any dinner that night.

Exploring the island next morning was a huge adventure. After a visit to Peel to view the castle and the House of Mannanan, I was starting to absorb the unique history of the Isle. I visited a Celtic roundhouse, saw a Viking long ship, the obnoxious smell of a herring processing plant assailed my senses, and I discovered what it was like to live in a Viking longhouse. After a lunch of Queenies (tiny Manx scallops) we set off for the Calf of Man. Salty thick fog and drizzle swirled around us, we were forced to drive with windows down, lights on, and were constantly on alert for oncoming vehicles. Unsurprisingly we met no one. Arriving at a remote crossroads there were no road signs. Chuckling, I asked if they were still expecting a German invasion and I began to wonder if the Manx had not realised the war was over. Deciding to turn right we crept along the narrow roads as the fog thickened and getting lost became a real possibility. I hoped we would not find ourselves on jagged rocks after driving over a remote cliff or attached by crushed metal to a huge stone wall. I had not planned on a hospital visit or a rest in the morgue. Eventually our destination loomed ahead, the small village of Cregneash where we visited a national folk museum which consists mainly of an original thatched Manx village. The rooms were smoke filled, basic and would have been very cold. A woman dressed in period costume took us to see the blacksmith and introduced me to a very nervous Manx cat. At the café my large cup of delicious coffee was adorned with the three-legged Manx symbol. Travelling back to Ramsey I noticed many of the corners were still sandbagged from the TT races held three weeks previously. As the watery sun silently appeared, we visited Tynwald, the site of the oldest continuous parliamentary body in the world. Preparations were being made for Tynwald Day to be held the following month.

Next day it poured incessantly! After a quick stop to view the Laxy wheel, where I got drenched, we carefully avoided the horse tramway in Douglas and dived into a warm inviting café for thick spicy tomato soup and toast. An unexpected text confirmed that despite the storm the ferry was definitely sailing. I left clutching a Women's Institute calendar.

Several months later while doing some detailed genealogical research on my father's family, I discovered I had distant relatives on the Isle of Man, Viking blood may run through my Celtic veins.

Mannan Museum

No Take Away from Cuenca
by Valerie Fletcher Adolph

We ate lunch in the shade of Cuenca's cathedral then strolled around the market where local women displayed vivid flowers and crafts.

I coveted the flowers. I wanted buckets full of red, purple, orange flowers. Ridiculous! Buckets of flowers don't fit in backpacks.

We headed down the main street where a mixture of businesses and homes opened right on to the sidewalk. We stopped at a panama hat factory to watch hats being made. At the insistence of the saleslady we tried on a few.

"How beautiful you look!" "It suits you perfectly!" "You'll be the centre of attention in this hat!"

Well, yes, I would be the centre of attention at my grandson's hockey rink wearing a panama hat.

Reluctantly I relinquished the opportunity of becoming beautiful. I wandered along soaking up the architecture, colours, sounds and smells of Cuenca. Suddenly an imposing carved door opened beside us. A woman dressed like a bygone European peasant hissed "You must come in."

She was no more than four feet tall, clad in a shawl and long black dress, her wiry hair pulled into a bun.

"You must come in," she repeated. "Madame said."

We stood, uncertain, gob smacked. She reached out and pulled the nearest person (me) inside. To my huge relief the others followed.

We stood at the foot of a curving staircase with old-style portraits covering the walls. At the top, beckoning us, was a tall, commanding woman, dressed as an eighteenth-century dowager French queen might dress.

Presumably this was Madame.

Her voice was deep and heavily-accented, "Welcome!" She gestured for us to climb the thickly carpeted staircase. As the last of our small group began the ascent the peasant woman closed the door to the street. I heard her lock it.

Madame led us into a dining room where a long table was set for twenty people. I wondered if we were to dine here. None of us could afford it.

She set our minds at rest. This was merely part of the normal furnishings. Madame reached for a switch and ornate chandeliers shone down from an intricately-ornamented ceiling to reveal exquisite china and glassware, carved chairs with immaculate velvet seats. We might have been in Versailles.

Large portraits stared disapprovingly from the walls. Moving from left to right Madame named each of the subjects, relating each grand duke, prince, admiral, black sheep and delicate countess to herself. Occasionally she hinted at salacious details or eyebrow-raising malfeasance. She named names across centuries from Medicis to tsars, from Holy Roman Emperors to Napoleon's Josephine. All connected, she said, to her family.

Then we were led to a lounge, similarly opulent and with portraits on the walls. Had she missed any grand duke, Infanta or archbishop? More names, more titles. As our eyes glazed over Madame said, "Next I will show you my bedroom."

Ready for the next onslaught of major and minor royalties with perhaps some titillating gossip we followed her. I was surprised to find her bedroom was no exotic boudoir but the size of a child's room. It contained a single bed, desk, a crucifix on the wall and brown linoleum on the floor.

"I live very simply," she said. I wondered where she hid the wardrobe that contained her elaborate gown, her long black gloves and her jewellery. Before I could ask, she said "Now! For my treasures!"

Not more ancestors, please! She led us into what looked like a small classroom, full of glass cases crammed with South American artifacts. Unlike the pristine condition of other rooms everything here was covered in dust. She pointed out major pieces. Almost all were pre-Columbian, some pre-Incan.

And while I had wondered about the veracity of her connections to European royalty, I believed her provenance of the South American artifacts. It was in the details, in the tone of her voice, in her look of reverence.

I wondered if we were expected to buy these, but she said "These are national treasures. I cannot, I would not, sell any of them."

Sigh of relief.

Then Madame turned to the display cases in the centre of the room, also containing artifacts.

"These," she said, waving a dismissive hand "Are forgeries. Very good forgeries, but forgeries nonetheless. Only an expert could tell the difference."

I thought I might perhaps afford a forgery. Most were small and would fit into my backpack. This must have been the purpose of our rather unusual hijacking.

Janie, next to me, pointed to a squat fertility goddess. "How much is she?"

Madame laughed. It wasn't her rich European royalty laugh, it was the laugh of someone who understood forgeries.

"I can't sell these either. They are too good. If a customs man found that in your luggage, he'd think it was genuine. It's against the law to take artifacts out of Ecuador. You would be in jail."

We gazed for a long time at artifacts, real and forged, as Madame detailed the history and culture of each one. She gave life and dimension to Pre-Columbian culture.

Then Madame seemed to tire. She guided us to the curved staircase at the foot of which stood the peasant woman. The door was closed, keys in her hand.

Here it comes, I thought.

In broken English she explained that Madame needed to charge visitors to see around her treasures. I mentally counted the local currency I had. This could be expensive.

She named a ridiculously small amount, the equivalent of $2. It would not sustain anyone very long.

We all paid up. Did it help Madame, or did it go straight into the peasant woman's apron pocket?

She unlocked the door and we stepped out onto the street where a noisy pre-election parade was passing.

I had nothing to show for the day - no flowers, no panama hat, no forged artifact. No take away at all.

Bali Ha'i
by Roger Knight

Bali Ha'i will whisper
in the wind of the sea,
'Here am I, your special island!
Come to me, come to me!'

Rogers and Hammerstein's South Pacific

My quest for Bali Ha'i finally came to fruition, after flying from Brisbane to Port Vila, followed by an internal flight, and then about a three-hour catamaran trip, to eventually reach Bokisa island, in the South Pacific island nation of Vanuatu, located 10 km south of Espiritu Santo.

Given its isolation and pristine setting, the coral and shell strewn beach, scattered, like so many jewels of the sea, the clear warm water and dense vegetation, quickly became my special island. A veritable Bali Ha'i found.

My purpose for being there, was ostensibly to dive the wreck of the luxury liner and troop ship from the second world war, the SS President Coolidge, considered to be one of the best full penetration wreck dives in the world, at nearly 200m long and 25m wide in size.

The island resort was managed by an Australian and Japanese couple. He was the dive master and she took me on preparatory dives, to determine if I was really up to diving the Coolidge. The first dive with her, resulted in an unexpected encounter with dozens of circling reef sharks. Her response was just to kneel on the sea floor until the sharks eventually swam away. Her composure in the face of significant threats, certainly impressed me at the time.

After that, she took me on a wreck dive, on a freighter in a depth of about 30m. All went well, until I swam straight into the face of a giant grouper, who had made his home in the stern of the ship. Fortunately, I was able to extricate myself, before encroaching further into his territory.

Having now been assessed as competent enough to dive the Coolidge and not pose a dive risk, on what could be a tricky dive, requiring decompression stops, I was ready to fulfil my purpose for being there.

On the morning we headed out to the wreck, there was just the divemaster, me and two Japanese divers. As we geared up, the two Japanese divers, donned head bands with Japanese script on them. They reminded me of what Kamikaze pilots used to wear on their suicide missions, and I wondered what their purpose might be in this context. Later into the dive, which was around 30 mins, we swam into a cavernous cargo hold, full of jeeps and aircraft equipment, whereupon, one of the Japanese divers struck the bottom of the hold with his fins, kicking up the accumulated silt, resulting in a sudden loss of visibility.

At this stage, we were now low on air and couldn't wait for the visibility to improve. Fortunately, our dive master knew the wreck like the back of his hand and he managed to grope around, until he had located the exit. Needless to say, we were not diving on a reel of line. For a few anxious moments, I thought that we might end up being entombed with all the unused jeeps and aircraft refuelling tanks.

I still wonder to this day, if that incident was in anyway linked to why they wore their head bands, and what agenda if any they had, by wearing them.

My second dive was not as eventful, but equally exhilarating, as the following piece of prose might attest to and which hopefully conveys the essence of the experience.

Finning down through the deep blue expanse of the South Pacific, the stricken ship comes into view. Lying like a fallen colossus, in recumbent repose on the sea floor. A significant casualty of war.

The luxury liner, turned troopship, is now a haven to a myriad of sea creatures. New life has emerged from her sinking. No longer carrying passengers, she provides sanctuary to permanent residents, with no class distinction.

Swimming through her holds and decks, the debris of warfare lies randomly scattered, bearing testament to the purpose of her final voyage.

This historical event, although frozen in time, has become shrouded in a patina of soft corals, marine growth and sediment, and I feel, that I have entered some eerie underwater catacomb, although only two souls perished.

Venturing further into one of the main holds, crammed with jeeps, one of the Japanese divers, strikes the bottom, laden with silt and visibility is instantly lost. Luckily our dive master is still able to locate the exit and we escape potential entombment.

Our dive time is almost up, and as we ascend for our deco stop, the ship fades from view, disappearing into the opaque blue, making this historical visit, seem like a dissipating dream.

Having dived on wrecks in several locations around the world, this would have to be the holy grail of diving.

Back on Bokisa, I returned to my hut, with its thatched palm roof and woven bamboo walls, which inside had several resident reptiles, that helped to keep the insect population under control.

Reflecting on my two dives on the Coolidge, I felt perhaps like a mountaineer, having reached the summit of a challenging peak, despite the inherent risks involved. In a sense too, I felt privileged to have been able to visit a piece of relatively undisturbed history, that will eventually evanesce, not unlike other such famous wrecks like the Titanic.

As for spending the rest of my life on Bokisa island, the thought does still tempt me from time to time.

The Ladies of the Lake
by Bonnie Jean Warren

The unpaved path from Kalaw to Inle Lake in the hills of Northern Myanmar offers great adventure to those seeking to be swept into another realm. An overnight trek, passing rice fields and peripatetic deer is a feast for the eyes, distracting from the head-splitting heat of rural Myanmar.

Powering through our water bottles, our nomadic tour group, consisting only of four and a tour guide, take rest in a wooden house propped precariously on the edge of a jagged rock formation. We are greeted at the door by May, a stout woman with a smile warmer than the sun, who prepares for us platters of unusual fruit that we fail to pronounce and, of course, tea.

Once we are fully rested, May sees us out of her home to sojourn across the hills passing clay villages where elderly seamstresses spindle thread. We are now entering Paoh territory, signified by the women wearing hand-woven red scarves on their heads. Pausing in one of the huts of a village, two children dash past.

"How old are the children?" I ask the guide who translates in local dialect to the seamstress.

"She guesses about 4 and 7 years old," he replies.

Here, time is irrelevant. Coming from bustling New York City, I struggle to fathom what it would be like to not live for time. Beside the seamstress lies a basket full of red scarves. She hands them to us and we offer her our change as gratitude before bidding her adieu. She glances at the currency without a care before diligently returning to work.

"The Paoh people believe that a female and male dragon flew across Myanmar during a storm. The male dragon got lost and when the female stopped at Inle Lake, she turned into a lady incapable of falling asleep," the guide continues as the four of us fight the oppressive heat across the fields, watching the Dragon ladies tend to their crops.

This was their daily routine. The Paoh people rarely stray far from their homes, having built their own communities from the resources available at their fingertips. Captivated by their religious beliefs, I hung on the guide's every word as he continued.

"The lady then met a frog who led her to a cave where she met a meditating shaman. She pretended to be human because she loved the

186

shaman and thought he wouldn't accept her for the dragon she was. Four years later, the shaman and dragon lady married. The dragon lady fell pregnant with twins. One day, while the shaman was in town, the dragon lady was exhausted and fell asleep. She turned back into a dragon. When the shaman came back, he was furious that she lied about who she was. He ran away and never came back."

The guide led us down a rocky terrain, passing by a shallow creek cascading down the hill to the lake. A cave to the right prompted my imagination of the dragon and the shaman.

"Heartbroken, the lady begged the frog to be human, to take her to the shaman again, but the frog said she couldn't have a second chance. After laying her eggs, she flew back to the dragon world. Paoh monks found these eggs and they tell this story to their tribe. The women wear the red scarves on their heads to symbolize the dragon's breath."

On the outskirts of another nearby village, we pass three of the women wandering up a steep hill effortlessly with their bamboo baskets of crops for dinner.

Suddenly, a snake jutted out from the bushes to my left and all three women hiss in unison.

"Careful! This snake is very poisonous!" The guide urged.

One of the women races past me and spears her stick instantly at the snake, piercing its skull into the dirt. The women cheer as our tour group observes mortified.

We help the ladies carry their baskets back to our residence for the evening, a large wooden room with a thin mat on the ground and four pillows and blankets laid out for us. The room is sparse, the village lacking in facilities. Rain is collected for water and there is no flush in the outhouse.

Once the sun sets over the meadows, we are cast into complete darkness. A silence sweeps over the landscape as the town goes to bed.

I'm left to comprehend living without a definitive schedule or the distractions of social media to while away the hours. I am lulled to sleep by the percussion of the wooden window against the frame in the breeze, a change from the tapping of my phone as I scroll through Instagram. A series of stars are my nightlight for the evening, a welcome change from Netflix.

In a realm far, far away, I was uncovering the magic of simplicity and awakening my inner Dragon lady.

Ladies of the lake

The Long Way There
by Ronald Mackay

The most direct route to any destination may be the fastest but it's unlikely to be the most interesting.

When, in 1974, I was offered an appointment in Mexico City, I was living in England. I consulted my atlas. The most direct route would be from London to Mexico by plane. About 12 hours non-stop. I looked at the wide Atlantic and then the expanse of North America. I'd have to fly the ocean given that trans-Atlantic passenger ships were becoming a thing of the past, but I wasn't going to miss all of that glorious North America!

And so I boarded the flight from London to Washington DC – a trip of a mere seven hours and then bought a ticket on the Greyhound Bus from Washington DC to Laredo in Texas. The kind of ticket that allowed me to break my journey at any point for a night or two and then resume it without any additional cost.

Now I didn't leave Washington right away. I wasn't going to let that gem pass! So I spent two days enjoying organised tours to all of the sights and then visited a friend in Georgetown. The morning I was to meet him at the University it snowed. That charming city on the Potomac with its sober federal architecture and its quaint streets delighted me as I alighted from the taxi, careful not to slip on the cobbles lightly-covered in snow.

It was just before nine, but the university campus struck me as lifeless. At the wrought-iron gates, I asked the security guard for directions. He looked at me cautiously.

"What time's your appointment?"

"Nine o'clock,"

"Not today, it ain't!"

I looked at him, wondering.

"It's snowing!"

I looked at the gentle covering of snow and the odd snowflake drifting down light as a feather.

"It snows here! Everything's cancelled!"

That was my first taste of the southern distaste for what we in the UK took in our stride as the natural accompaniment to winter.

* * *

"You can't take the Greyhound to Mexico City!" David's voice was incredulous or disapproving – or more likely both.

"Only as far as Laredo," I told him. "Then I walk across the bridge and buy a ticket in Nuevo Laredo from the Mexican bus-line that will take me on South.

He shook his head. He was an educated man and knew about 'mad dogs and Englishmen'.

* * *

In the cheapest hotel I could find in the French Quarter, I stopped for two nights in New Orleans. Even that economy left me low on funds. Having walked Bourbon Street that first night scanning the expensive menus, I plumped for an Italian restaurant. Elegant though it was, one dish had caught my eye as the most inexpensive of all I'd seen.

"Spaghetti a la naturale." It sounded simple. And healthy. And it was very, very cheap.

I went in. I sat down. The waiter greeted me, pen poised.

With the most cosmopolitan flourish I could muster to give the impression it was my most favoured of dishes, I ordered. "Spaghetti a la naturale."

His pencil did not move. His lips did. "And?"

"That's all!"

"Spaghetti a la naturale. That's it?"

"That's it!" I smiled. "Spaghetti a la naturale. My favourite meal!" He nodded barely suppressing a smirk.

Ten minutes later he placed a deep white plate of spaghetti in front of me and retired to the kitchen. I waited for the delivery of whatever accompaniment came with it.

And waited.

And Waited.

"Is everything to your liking, Sir?" He'd returned and was looking pointedly at my untouched plate.

Then the translation kicked in. I had ordered 'simply spaghetti' – nothing more and nothing less. He saw my confusion, guessed the cause and kindly showed me how to dress the simple dish with olive oil and parmesan. When I finished that cheapest of meals, he removed my empty plate placed a large green salad in front of me.

190

"On the house!"

In the kitchen, they were dying of laughter at the impecunious Scot whose favourite meal was boiled spaghetti!

* * *

Three days it took me to cross the border from Laredo into Nuevo Laredo. Despite presenting my passport and the accompanying credentials that attested to my appointment at the National Autonomous University of Mexico, the furtive official kept finding something wrong with them, though he was unable to explain what.

The Border Agent on the American side took me aside. He'd seen me make my unsuccessful attempt one day after the other and watched me walk back over the bridge, suitcases in each hand.

"You don't know what's missing?" He looked at me amazed.

"No idea!"

"You got a twenty?" He showed me how to fold it into my passport. "You jes go on back there an your troubles is over!"

And they were.

I made the trip to Mexico City in stages, fascinated by the revelation that I'd tumbled two centuries backwards when I'd crossed the Rio Grande. Though in the most picturesque of ways.

On the last stage in the spartan long-distance bus, the two drivers entertained the passengers by replacing each other for rest spells without reducing the outrageous speed of their bus. Delighted passengers clapped as one driver took steering-wheel, then accelerator, then seat from his exhausted partner as we barrelled down the white line scattering donkeys.

Yes, that trip taught me that the most interesting route to any destination is definitely not the simplest!

A Jungle River in Darkness
by Delores Topliff

My wristwatch read 3 a.m. as my 14-year-old son and I joined those in the large dugout canoe to head upriver. We'd been in Colombia three months helping communities along this Amazon tributary where I taught classes and did teacher training, and my son swung a machete to help men clear fields.

When our ninety-day visa expired, our expected renewal was refused because of increased guerrilla activity. In fact, Colombia's Army closed the Caquetá River to travel and imposed military curfew. Occasional daytime traffic was allowed by permit, but none at night.

Aaron and I came before conditions got so bad. To leave, we must reach the small river town of Curillo where a narrow-rutted road headed north to civilization.

There, a daily open-air jeep carried passengers and livestock to a larger town for the twelve-hour bus ride across the Andes to Bogotá.

Soldiers patrolled relentlessly. We asked the Army's Commandant for special travel permission. He refused until he understood our situation. "Perhaps if you shine flashlights on your faces to show you are not guerillas." He laughed and promised to send word to his sentries. We hoped for reliable batteries.

At 3 a.m. we loaded and our laboring outboard pushed us upstream. But this sixteen-week trip actually began years earlier when my son and I lived with a family moving to Colombia. Once they got settled, we stayed in touch by letters and ham radio. Their daughters, Shannon and April, now 17 and 18, became teachers creating a school where there had been none.

Over ham radio, they asked if I could send textbooks for math, history, and English. When I did, my students wrote accompanying letters, the first the Colombian pupils had ever received. We described our farms with log homes in a land of ice and snow and woods full of moose and bear. Carmen, age nineteen, had just learned to read and write. At ninety, Serafino could write but had never received a letter. They drew colorful pictures and wrote letters my friends translated from Spanish. They described bamboo homes and their jungle river birthed in the towering Andes. They were sad we couldn't grow sugar cane or bananas so plentiful they fed them to their pigs. They hungered for the potatoes we grew by the ton.

In more radio conversations, April and Shannon said it would be even better if I could come and train teachers. I said I would love to, but as a volunteer myself, I had little income.

My school followed these messages, and over the next six months, I received enough donations for my younger son and I to make the trip. We rode Greyhound from the Pacific Northwest to Miami, and then two planes, one bus, and the large open jeep to reach the remote jungle where Colombia, Peru, and Ecuador meet. For three full months we helped communities along this river running east to Brazil. All transportation was by foot or motorized canoe.

We came to help these people, but they blessed us more. Children climbed trees to bring clusters of magnificent orchids, bright butterflies the size of dinner plates, the polished ear bones of a giant fish, and a twenty-two-foot Anaconda skin. One pregnant woman walked six miles on muddy trails carrying her two-year-old to hear me speak. I prayed for inspiring words for people making such effort.

With our visa renewal denied but the river closed, how could we leave?

We knew a guerrilla base operated two miles away. Some people walking along a riverbank daily or through our camp were guerrillas. Clothing disappeared from clotheslines and food from our kitchens.

That's why Colombia's Army now held and controlled the river. They praised our early morning routine when we gathered to start the day drinking homegrown coffee and singing hymns before we worked in gardens or taught school in the cool part of the day. Once the sun became a furnace, we ate a large meal and performed less demanding chores. Army officials concluded it was our singing that gave unity to our communities of blended nationalities.

"We know your secret," their captain confided. He made his troops stand in formation each morning to sing songs. Their practice was shown on national T.V. but didn't achieve the desired results. We decided it mattered what they sang.

One man visited our community for a week and left a note warning that he was a spy planning an upcoming guerrilla attack. We were vulnerable. The simple bamboo homes had open windows with no glass. Many walls were only waist high. Most doors had no locks. We were politically neutral, helping all who came. But as tensions between the Army and the guerrillas worsened, we needed to leave.

One loving grandmother had often asked my help for her severely burned grandson who had fallen into a fire. She sang to him daily, stretching his limbs and applying salve to lessen his pain. I had promised to visit again but had been busy with students and now time had run out.

On this last day, when I entered her gate, she wept and spoke blessings. "God bless you with strength and love and peace always for you, your children and their children forever." She threw her apron over her head as sobs overtook her.

Sobs overtook me, too, as we hugged.

And then came darkness and fitful sleep before Aaron and the rest of us boarded the canoe. It is eerie to travel jungle rivers at night and hear animal and other noises on shore but see nothing. Time moves very slowly. We were thankful forty minutes later to reach the river town of Curillo.

As we docked, we thanked the Commandant for giving us travel permission, so we could connect with the once-a-day jeep. He told us that he had forgotten to pass on our travel permit, but when his sentries saw us shining lights on our faces, they decided that we were harmless and held their fire.

Downhill on a Bike in Bali
by Brigid Gallagher

The highlight of my first trip to the Indonesian island of Bali was way out of my comfort zone.

Indeed, I questioned my sanity at setting out on a Downhill Eco Bike Tour, on the singular recommendation of a **seventy**-year-old tourist, for I had not been astride a bicycle for more than fifteen years!

The great day arrived, and I was collected from my *homestay* accommodation in the village of Nyuh Kuning and joined a small group of others on a trip north to Kintamani, a town overlooking Mount Batur, an active volcano rising to 1717m.

The vast lava fields from the eruption of 1968 could be viewed from our first stop – a local restaurant. Mount Batur last erupted in 2000, and I wondered if it would produce a crackling display as we ate breakfast.

Thankfully, we escaped unscathed!

A visit to a Luwak coffee plantation followed, where a poor Asian palm civet consumes coffee berries, digests and ferments them internally, before defecating them into a new more *aromatic* form. Luwak coffee is known as "The World's Most Expensive Coffee."

Indeed, Jack Nicholson and Morgan Freeman's ashes were placed on either side of a tin of this *delicacy*, atop a Himalayan Mountain in one of my favourite movies – "The Bucket List."

Leaving the coffee plantation behind, we stopped once again, before beginning the highlight of our trip – the downward descent...

Our tour guide equipped us with bicycles of the right size, helmets for our safety, and bottles of water to prevent dehydration. Meanwhile, a lovely Australian couple gave me great tips on the intricacies of gear changing, before our little group set off on smooth, tarred roads that were thankfully free of traffic.

Throughout the bike ride, we encountered only an occasional scooter, but LOTS of smiling children cheered us all along our route. Thankfully, I had a minder – a second tour guide - who kept a good watch over me and added to my education on the laws of gear changing!

Feeling more relaxed, I actually began to enjoy myself. However, I remained at the rear of the group for the first half of our trip.

"We will stop here," my minder announced, as we joined the others outside a village house. The owners welcomed us inside a series of small buildings, somewhat less affluent than my accommodation back in Nyuh Kuning.

"These stones guard the family member's placentas and will protect them throughout their lives," he announced.

The rear of the compound held a garden, planted with neat rows of vegetables and a few flowers. The shade provided a welcome retreat from the sun for a family of chickens and two suckling pigs, which looked over a stone pig pen with *imploring* eyes. Sadly, they lead a very short life as suckling pig is considered an essential ingredient in traditional Balinese ceremonies.

Rural villagers are largely self-sufficient, supplementing home-grown vegetables, chicken and pork with locally grown rice. The rice paddies were our next stop.

Here we learned of the length of the growing season – three in a year- the irrigation system known as *subak*, and the organic method of fertilisation, using ducklings to manure the fallow paddies, whilst fattening them up for the gastronomic delights of Balinese smoked or crispy duck. Incidentally, everyone who works in the rice paddies shares in the season's crops, although the landowner gets the largest portion.

As we stood amidst the paddies, having stepped over subak streams and slippery clods of earth, to delight in the endless green landscape, I had a burning question and asked, "Are there many snakes in the rice paddies?"

The reply was brief. "The farmer kills them every morning."

Later, we witnessed a poor, muddy worker ploughing a flooded paddy field with a large version of a garden rotavator. We learned that he earned around 7 euro for ploughing a field of ten square metres – considered a small fortune by Balinese standards.

I wondered how many snakes he encountered each day?

Our tour continued.

The next stop was a village temple, filled with beautiful Balinese ladies, all chatting and laughing, as they created floral offerings for the temple. I delighted in photographing them in their rainbow of traditional lace tops and sarongs.

My energy levels were flagging, and I was now wilting from the heat. I silently wondered, "Are we there yet?"

Thankfully, "The End" was in sight.

I breathed a sigh of relief as VERY welcome iced face flannels were distributed, and a discussion followed...

"Do you want to go for lunch now, or do you want to continue for another 8km UPHILL?"

Guess which option I chose?

Six of my travelling companions voted for the lunch NOW option, while two younger energetic cyclists chose the extended route. Ten minutes later, our group descended on a lovely restaurant, complete with its own organic vegetable garden, and delighted in a feast fit for royalty.

The uphill team joined us later, obviously the worse for wear!

Temple Ladies

Tambo Viejo means The Old Inn in Quechua
by Mark Boyter

This is a story about Peru. Or Me. Or friends. Or synchronicity.

It's about something.

You can decide.

It was 2001. February. Or January. Who can remember these things, especially after a few beers? Besides, the month is not important to the story, whether it is about me or a friend or synchronicity or just about being about.

I was in Arequipa, Peru. A UNESCO World Heritage city. Already old when Pizarro's men arrived in 1540. In the south, on the edge of the Andes. A religious city, but that seems redundant in Peru. Everything feels religious here, everywhere spiritual. Sometimes it's Catholic. Sometimes it's Incan. Sometimes it's Moche. Sometimes it's Shamanic. Sometimes it's all.

I had arrived in Peru, to the tiny north coastal town of Las Delicias, on December 3 to visit DS, an American friend from grad school. My birthday. That I remember. Not all dates are fluid. Transitions matter.

I had been working long distance with DS on his thesis; the idea that the stages of acculturation mirror Kübler-Ross's stages of grief in death and dying, that to take on a new culture meant the death of the old one, and in all death, there is grief. The deeper the acquisition, the more intense the immersion, the deeper the loss: of familiarity, of history, of touchstones. Of self.

I needed to see Las Delicias.

DS was a shaman. A good shaman. A *curandero*. Not a *brujo*. He had come to learn from Eduardo Calderón, "El Tuno", and never left. Eduardo lived on the poor side of town. Eight kilometers from Trujillo, just off the Pan-American Highway. From Las Delicias, all directions were possible.

I stayed almost a month, helping finish the thesis, learning Spanish, taking on new rhythms. In Las Delicias only DS spoke English; Trujillo was not much better. Little was familiar, and slowly but ineluctably, I began to embody DS's thesis. I made it through all five stages. Again, and again. There is no end. The line isn't linear but spiral.

While Eduardo's curanderism was traditional, DS brought the West, and over many beers he talked about Jungian psychology and how it resonated and informed his pathway. Synchronicity and the architypes especially, but in synchronicity there seemed something I could grasp. I can thank Sting for that. I wanted to understand. To know. I brought two books with me: Jung's *Synchronicity*, and *Synchronicity: Science, Myth, and the Trickster* by Combs and Holland.

On January 1, I left to head south. That date too I remember. Transitions.

In Arequipa I wanted to see Santa Catalina Convent, a walled 16th C Dominican enclave that had been closed to the outside world for 400 years, and across the Rio Chili, La Recoleta, a 17th C Franciscan monastery. La Recoleta was famous for its collection of manuscripts, but I was mostly curious to compare monks to nuns. The library was a bonus.

In the morning on my way to Santa Catalina, I passed the Don Quixote café. Not an unusual name for a Spanish café and I didn't stop, but I found myself singing the Nik Kershaw song "Don Quixote" for the rest of the day. Nik had been my soundtrack to Europe in 1984. It was nice to have him back, to remember.

Hidden behind high white-washed walls, Santa Catalina's inner alleys and rooms and cloisters were painted in the most rich and vibrant blues and pinks and ochres, and my short visit turned to long hours. It was not until past mid-day that I made it across the river to La Recoleta. It was, by contrast, spartan and white and cold. The library was up a thick wooden staircase. The rarest manuscripts were in a long glass bookcase running the middle of the book room. In the center, a monk told us, was a 1647 first South American edition of Cervantes' *Don Quixote*.

In February, or perhaps January, in southern Peru it grows dark early, and at altitude, biting. I made my way back to my inn, wrote for a while, and then took out the Combs' book and started to read. Again. I'd started Combs a few times in Las Delicias, but found it unengaging each time before putting it aside.

I had, years earlier, a similar experience with another book, *Chaos*. I'd read chapter one, get half way through chapter two, lose the rhythm, force the text, understand nothing, give up, and put it aside, only repeat and repeat *ad* God love me *nauseum*.

One day I decided to just open *Chaos* random and read. Chaos in action, as it were. Perhaps the logical flow that I thought the book demanded was all in my imagination. Perhaps chaos was as much a suggestion as a title.

And it worked.

The book still bored me, but that's not the point. At least I don't think that's the point.

I decided to try the same with *Synchronicity*. So in that cold, dark, Arequipan room, I opened a page somewhere in the middle and started to read.

The passage was about two middle-aged twin sisters who were cleaning out their father's library after his death. The library was large, with ladders on rails to reach the highest books. At one point, one sister picked up a book on one side of the library only to discover that her sister, on the other side of the library at that same moment, in total unawareness, had picked up a second copy of that same book. Cervantes' *Don Quixote*.

And I closed the book, turned off the light, and went downstairs for dinner and a beer.

When I got home to Vancouver, I related the story to a friend. He had once lived in Spain.

"Why," he asked, "did you sing the Nik Kershaw song, and not the Gordon Lightfoot song "Don Quixote"?

I stayed friends with him for many years after that.

I don't know why.

We all, I suppose, need friends. Any friend.

Through Their Eyes
by Lindsay de Feliz

I had been living in the Dominican Republic for a year and had a return ticket to England which had to be used within the year, so I decided to go back to the UK for a couple of weeks and as I had enough points, I also decided to take my then boyfriend, now husband, with me. He had never left the DR, so amidst great excitement, we sorted all the paperwork for his visa and headed to the airport in Santo Domingo.I really had not considered what it would be like for someone who had never travelled. We arrived at the airport.

"Now where we go?" he asked.

"Check in," I replied.

"What is shecking?"

"It is where they take your luggage and weigh it and decide what seat you will have on the plane and give you your boarding pass."

We headed to check in, and I explained that the luggage had to go on the scales.

"Why they weigh luggage? "

"Because the pilot has to know how much weight the plane is carrying so he can put in the right amount of fuel," I replied patiently.

Danilo put the suitcase onto the scale and then jumped up next to it.

"What on earth are you doing?" exclaimed the check in lady.

"You need know how much I weigh," he replied.

I pulled him off the scales and we then had a long conversation in Spanish about the fact that they only weighed the luggage and not the people and that yes it was stupid and they should weigh the people first and yes thin people should be allowed to take more luggage than larger people but they were the rules.

I then had to stop him running to drag his luggage off the conveyor belt as he thought he would never see it again and couldn't believe it would be waiting for him in London and eventually we boarded the plane having had to pay the man at immigration US$100 when he said the visa was probably false and it would take a couple of days to check it – unless we paid up and then he would know it was not a fake visa.

As he was looking open mouthed at all of the buttons, and the television screen, Danilo asked, "When will my mouth go around to my ears? Chi Chi said (a friend who knows everything) that is what happens when you fly, as it is so fast".

The questions were nonstop and eventually, having changed planes in Madrid, we arrived in London.

We reached immigration and he whispered, "How much do I have to pay lady?"

"Nothing, there is no corruption in England. You don't bribe anyone."

The immigration lady was fine and allowed me to translate and we were through in no time but for the first time ever in my life we were stopped and searched by customs, and this was to happen in the future every time we flew together. Profiling at its best.

We reached the hotel, The Mad Hatter in Waterloo in London, or as he called it, The Crazy Hat, and having checked in we went to our room. In the corridor outside was a shoe shine machine.

"What is that?" he asked.

"A shoe shine machine," I replied.

"Nooooo. Shoe shine is young boy not machine," as he checked out how to shine his shoes which had to be done every time he passed the machine.

He had never seen a bath, never used hot water to bath or shower and came running out of the bathroom with toilet paper in his hand, "There is no bin for the paper," he hissed.

"Put it in the toilet, we don't use bins in England,"

"Nooo it will block. No want block toilet."

"It won't block we have thick pipes here."

He was awestruck wandering around London, having never seen a double decker bus (we always had to sit upstairs and duck every time we went under a bridge), never been on an escalator, a train, a tube train and had a total melt down on the Docklands Light Railway.

"There is no driver!"

"No it is driven by a computer."

"But what if electricity goes? "

"It won't. This is England. The electricity never goes."

The pressing of the pedestrian button to cross the road was accompanied by great excitement waiting for the little green man to appear on the other side.

"Hombre verde, hombre verde!" he would shout, causing other pedestrians to smile or giggle.

The train journey to my parents' home in the country was peppered with squeals of delight every time he saw a rabbit in the fields. There he was amazed that the pigs had little houses and the horses wore coats and that the ducks on the duck pond had not been shot and eaten.

He couldn't get over that white smoke came out of his mouth when he blew out (it was cold), and that some thatched houses had "grass" on the roof – just like the palm leaves in the Dominican Republic.

He wore four pairs of underpants as ChiChi had told him his willy would shrink due to the cold, and couldn't understand why the chickens for sale in the supermarket had no feet on them.

Watching him and being with him in London was like being on a journey with a cross between ET and Crocodile Dundee. I have never laughed so much or looked at things in a different way and realised that those who are able to travel freely to so many places and experience so many cultures, without the need for visas, really are blessed.

A Tete a Tete with a Tortoise
by Malcom D. Welshman

I am wary when the world's oldest living land animal trundles up to where I am sitting and attempts to lever himself over my outstretched legs. Having no desire to have my kneecaps crushed by 300 kg of giant tortoise, I whisper a friendly, 'Hello Jonathan.' and proceed to tickle his neck. That does the trick. He comes to a halt, levers himself up on his front legs, neck outstretched, head held high. Bliss.

'Well, matey, I wonder how many times you've enjoyed having this done to you,' I say, as Jonathan turns his head and gives me a rheumy-eyed stare. After all, this tortoise is 186 years old.

My meeting has come about as a result of a speaking engagement I had on board a cruise ship where one of the ports of call was going to be St Helena a tiny island in the middle of the South Atlantic, 1,200 miles from the African mainland and one of the remotest places on earth. My curiosity had been immediately aroused since I had read about its most famous resident, Jonathan, the Seychelles giant tortoise. A national symbol. Appearing on the island's postage stamps and on the local five pence coin.

How could I miss the opportunity of having a tete a tete with him? I arranged this through Debbie, the manager at Plantation House, the Governor's residence where Jonathan also resides in a paddock within the manicured grounds at the front of the house.

As I stepped off the ship's tender onto the tiny wharf of Jamestown the island's capital, I could imagine Jonathan as a mere 50-year-old, being hoisted ashore at the same spot back in 1882.

'Now, old fella,' I said, still stroking Jonathan's neck. 'You hit the news big time last year.'

It was all to do with a tortoise called Frederica brought to the island in 1991 as a mate for Jonathan. Since then, he's duly carried out his duties on a regular basis. Last October, Frederica had to be treated for a chipped shell when it was discovered she was a he. Oh dear. International headlines. 'Jonathan's Gay!' And Frederica was hastily renamed Freddie.

Debbie tells me that Jonathan is on a weekly food supplement consisting of fruit and vegetables from the Plantation House garden to which are added apples and pears. These latter two have to be imported. Seems he gets more fresh fruit and veg than most of the islanders.

'But that's no surprise, is it old chap?' I say. 'You're a V.I.P. — a very important patient.'

I lean across and rub my nose against his beak. All very friendly. No objections. Head out, he continues to listen to me blathering on. Seems his hearing is still excellent. I swivel to one side when Jonathan, having decided he's been tickled enough, lumbers forward seeking the sanctuary of some shade.

Interview over. I smile and pat his shell as he passes.

'You're a true gentleman,' I murmur. 'Long may you reign.'

Jonathan with Malcolm

TRAVEL HIGHLIGHTS

I Know What Heaven Looks Like
by Sarah Owens

Our guide smiles revealing perfect white teeth.

"Hello, my name is Heaven, welcome to Botswana."So that's what heaven looks like: lean blue-black limbs, long neck and a smooth handsome face. He poles our mokoro canoe parting the reeds of the Okavengo delta with a soft swish and calls to the other guides in his melodic voice. I lie against my rucksack and settle into a dream like state. Bright dragon flies dance above the surface catching droplets of water, sunlight blazing through their turquoise and emerald wings. My fingers brush creamy water-lilies as we glide by.

Monarchs of the Forest
by Ronald Mackay

We drove with the windows down, the better to enjoy the crisp air and the scent of the pine forest. In an hour we'd be back in the Distrito Federal and our rented house in El Pedregal.

Without warning the sun vanished. Thousands of drifting objects so obstructed our vision that I was forced to stop.

A volcanic eruption?

As I slid the stick into reverse, Pearl called out, "Butterflies, Ronald! Millions of orange and black butterflies!"

They clung to the windshield and to us even as we descended from the jeep.

"The migration of the monarch!"

"They're glorious!"

Just One Day
by Robyn Boswell

Blue, smudgy early morning light in Wells Beach, Maine. The grey clapboard houses standing shoulder to shoulder crowded the beach. So alien to my eyes, used to the South Pacific's clear, sharp colours. I wandered down the hard sand and dabbled my feet in the cold crispness of the Atlantic Ocean. Hours later, late afternoon, in bold, brash, noisy Los Angeles. I took a taxi to Santa Monica, wandered down the soft sand by the pier and paddled in the warm Pacific. My ocean, but still not my home. One day, two great oceans.

A Call of Nature
by Malcolm D. Welshman

My call of Nature came one moonlit night, the rocky ridges of southern Sudan awash with silver. I slipped out of our tent, careful not to wake my girlfriend and clambered up the slope.

My relief was short-lived when each side of me deep-throated snarls erupted. I hurtled back down to the tent. The snuffles followed.

I nudged Maxeen. 'Listen,' I hissed, rasping purrs just inches beyond the canvas. 'Leopards.'

She half-woke. 'Frogs,' she murmured drowsily and fell asleep again.

When we emerged the next morning, large pug marks encircled the tent.

'Bloody large frogs,' was all I could say.

A Taste of Time Travel
by Sunny Lockwood

My Peruvian taxi driver says the most popular soft drink in the nation is Inca Kola.

"What's it taste like?" I ask.

He smiles mysteriously, "Unforgettable."

Suddenly, despite historic churches and monuments, all I want is to taste Inca Kola.

I get my wish.

Inca Kola is yellow. Not pale yellow like lemonade. Piercing yellow like neon on a rainy night.

One sip and I'm immediately a child again, standing at our local grocery candy counter. Dusty sweetness. Excitement. Little kid giddiness. What time travel magic!

Another swallow and I understand. I get it.

Inca Kola tastes like bubble gum.

Big Bad Bikers
by Syd Blackwell

Easy rider and his momma
cruised the highway up to Glossa
felt the wind blow through their hair
wore cool shades to cut the glare
stopped to look whenever they liked
posed for pictures on the bike
ate bad pizza drank good beer
at some taverna near the pier
stopped for swims in turquoise bays
where naked tourists catch the rays
scooted home before the rain
riding wet is such a pain
lived this life so vulgar and raw
on a 50cc Yamaha

(Skopelos, Greece, July 1989)

Manta Safari
by Alyson Hilbourne

I adjusted my mask, dipped my head below the surface and was rewarded with a huge manta directly below me, its mouth open, wing tips upturned like an A380, silently cutting through the water.

Everywhere I turned more appeared, slicing the cloudy, plankton rich sea, dark shapes uncloaking as they came into view.

They were hard to count. Twenty, thirty, fifty of these ocean titans swam below us, oblivious of the tourists and marine biologists snorkelling above, as they gorged for a few short hours on the food bonanza brought in by the high tide.

(Hanifaru Bay, The Maldives)

Snake Charmer
by Alan Passey

Hey guys - We got this. She shouted at the window as they came dragging a dustbin and carrying a long stick.

We stuffed towels into the daylight streaming under the door just as the snake snuck by towards the adjoining outhouse.

It almost made it. Our saviour flipped the stick, hooking the snake into the bin and slamming the lid down tight as it climbed the wall.

We'll show this to Hank. She grinned. Local snake man.

At dinner, Hank appeared at the door. The snake curling around his hand.

He's real friendly, he said.

He couldn't have moved faster.

Nine Percent
by Valerie Fletcher Adolph

We were visiting the whisky country of northeastern Scotland, staying with a farmer who grew barley for the local distillery. One day we followed the whisky trail, at each distillery given a 'wee dram' and told about the distilling process. I learned that as whisky matured in barrels approximately 9% was lost to evaporation.

Later that evening in the farm kitchen our host brought out a large medicine bottle, full of deep golden-brown whisky. Each of us drank generously, toasting each other, the barley crop and Scotland.

Then our host explained, "That was part of the 9% ."

Otters by the Pier
by James Robertson

We finally arrived in Monterey.

Getting out of the car, I made my way from the carpark to a small beach beside a pier which stretched out into the bay. The sun setting cut through the dappled clouds, coating the sea in yellow. Waves lapped against the concrete pier. Gulls cawed overhead. Docked ships creaked as they swayed. But there was another sound. Squeaking perhaps.

I saw, writhing in the seaweed, a young sea otter. Nearby was its mother, lying on her back, scraping shells on her belly. The baby dived playfully, slinking amongst the kelp.

I was in awe.

Flushed with Success
by Barbara Hunt

Australian toilets are hotbeds for graffiti artists, so what a pleasant surprise it was when I used the pristine Japanese 'loos' at Narita Airport, Tokyo. What fascinated me was the selection of buttons on the handle to the right of the pedestal.

It had 'spray' and 'bidet' buttons, but the 'flushing sound' (dubbed 'otohime' – princess sound – after the Japanese folktale of Urashima Tarō) intrigued me.

Music makes white noise to help self-conscious women retain their dignity by masking those undesirable noises.

I did indeed feel like a princess when I emerged, head held high, my indiscretions disguised.

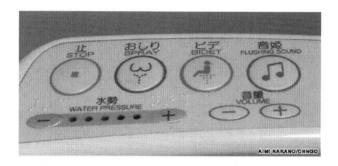

Jet-lag Doesn't Exist
by Ronald Mackay

Our organization forbad it.

We worked, then on to Schiphol. We returned, from where barely mentioned.

"Your task! Audit the EU initiative to reintroduce nutritious grains."

"Eastern Europe?"

"Bolivia, Ecuador and Peru. Quinoa, amaranth."

"That's it?"

"Millet in India and Nepal."

"How long?"

"Twenty days. Then a report To FAO in Rome."

"Right!"

No direct flights link India with Latin America. I chose Toronto as my hub.

Done!

Twenty-one separate flights; 4,200 Ks of trucking to villages. Looking, listening, asking, reading. Analysing, calculating, writing, confirming and rewriting.

Sleeping? Barely! But alert. The evaluator is always alert.

Jet-lag does not exist.

A whale pod sighting off Bermuda
by Roger Knight

Just off the south shore, thirty or so Sperm whales had gathered. I was immediately in awe of this marine mammal armada, lying as though at anchor, so close to the island.

They had enormous box like heads, that were squared off, and some were shooting columns of water high into the air through their blow holes, like a collection of geysers.

They all seemed to be in such gentle repose, despite appearing like some alien invasion force.

Day One on the Camino
by Hannah Standen

It's hard to tell if it the drops of water running down my face are sweat or rain.

It is pelting down, my boots squelch in the mud.

Counting to ten as I put one foot in front of the other. Repeat.

My body aches, I peer up the mountain, searching for the peak.

Thick fog surrounds me, I put my head back down.

One, two, three.

I am deep in concentration so do not hear him at first. 'Not long now' he repeats flashing a cheeky smile.

He powers past as I begrudgingly sigh, 'Only 29 days to go.'

Tea
by Vernon Lacey

'¿Hay té?' I ask the supermarket assistant. Is there tea?

'¿Como?'– *Pardon-* she says, puzzled.

I'm English. New in Spain. I'm pronouncing té the English way - *tea*.

'No entiendo,' the assistant says. *I don't understand.*

I improvise. 'Los ingleses – lo beben mucho.' *The English – they drink lots of it.* It's clumsy Spanish. I lift an imaginary teacup to my mouth.

Finally, the penny drops. '¡Ah! Si. Si,' the assistant says, all smiles. 'Ven conmigo.' *Come with me.*

She leads me to the back of the supermarket. There, to my shame, she points at the alcohol section.

Beach Daze, 1954
by Nancy McBride

Misquamicut Beach, RI: We'd ride a wonderful old carousal. Up and down, up and down, the painted horses lulled us around and around to the honky-tonk music of a calliope. Half of that time, we viewed the Atlantic gently lapping the shoreline.

Matunuck Beach, RI: We awoke being swallowed whole by a massive turbulent, hurricane-whipped tidal wave tearing us loose from our reality. Clinging to our cottage, now ark, we were viciously tossed, saturated, half-submerged, spinning around and around, no refuge in sight. Frantic and exhausted, we cheated death for interminable hours. No shoreline. Mayhem. And then...

Waking in Darjeeling
by Sarah Owens

The solemn sound of chanting wakes me. Softly at first it grows louder and louder until it crescendos with drums banging. I part the thin curtains and sunlight streams in. I catch my breath, Darjeeling bathed in a red glow from the early sun, sprawls out down the valley, prayer flags fluttering in the breeze. In the distance, the snow-tipped Himalayas gleam sharp against cobalt skies. The back-breaking journey to get here is forgotten. Throwing open the lattice windows, I lean out and breath pure mountain air.

Lithuanian Sauna
by Philip East

The heat is enveloping. With each thrash of doused birch on scorched rock a new wave of fire wrought steam catches in the throat, as pores are wrenched open and as filth and sweat glisten and pool.

I cannot stand it anymore.

Bursting out onto the manicured lawn I leap into the murky pond. One final suspension in the dying light of a sparkling Baltic Spring, the privet hedges and thick forest, the vegetable patch and chain link fence, the distant barking dog.

Then the fall.

Brief Encounter 1
by Dolores Banerd

Mosquitos? I've met many, but none were as excited to see me as the ones I encountered at a modest guesthouse in sleepy Nong Khai in northeast Thailand.

They laughed hysterically every time I slathered myself with repellent then buzzed with glee as they furiously attacked me gorging on my blood until bursting.

What's worse? They ruined my chances for a sizzling tryst with a new friend, a rakish Dutchman. Apparently, he was put-off by my incessant scratching, scratching, scratching and my body (once so luscious) with dozens of ugly red bumps failed to entice him. I'll never forgive them.

Basilica View
by James Robertson

Despite my claustrophobia I ascended the Esztergom Basilica; the largest church in Hungary.

Enclosed by ageing walls, I took each narrow step slowly.

Once I'd survived, the landscape met me warmly. Red-capped roofs jutted out of the tree-line. Boats dotted the shimmering surface of the Danube. The only bridge in sight crossed from Hungary to Slovakia. The neighbour melted into the horizon, conjoining fertile hills with the misty skyline.

My outlook was bookend by two blue domes, topped with crosses. I'm not religious. But no Atheist could deny the beauty that the Esztergom Basilica displays.

Shaky Isles
by Robyn Boswell

12am. Woke up as my bed slid backwards and forwards across the floor. Looked across the motel room at Julie sitting bolt upright in her bed. Said to her "Is this an earthquake?" No reply. Suddenly everything began to groan, crack and bang; cupboard doors crashed open and shut, open and shut. The beds kept sliding then juddered as they bounced up and down. The land roared. Eventually Julie said, "Is it supposed to last this long?" Slowly the movement stopped, and absolute silence reigned.

On reflection, a 7.8 was an overwhelming introduction to my first earthquake.

Autumnal Glory
by Malcolm D. Welshman

The forest cloaks me in the full splendour of its autumn's mantle. The burnished browns, golds and reds of the beeches. The sweet smell of their mast drifting with the falling leaves. The distant tap-tap of a woodpecker. A fallen log, decayed. A haven for fungi, red capped, polka-dotted white, tongues of caramel brown, cream-gilled. A stream rainbow-dances over a gravel bed. Diamonds of water sparkle and flash to vanish with a tinkling gurgle into a thicket of blue-green conifers. Within, a deep bed of pine needles carpet an emerald twilit grotto. Nature's magic is spellbinding. I stand entranced.

Border Smiles
by Ronald Mackay

"Our Passports."

Viviana tucks them into the truck papers. I concentrate, overtake long-distance transports returning to Bolivia and Brazil from Chile through Argentina.

"Check them?" We're into corkscrew bends; a tunnel; customs; immigration.

"The date's wrong! The permission's dated last year."

"Damn! Back! All that way!"

"They won't notice!"

"Officers are paid to notice."

"Not in Argentina!"

....

"Truck papers?" Uniformed scowls.

Viviana smiles. I squirm. Officers scrutinize, move lips.

"Such a beautiful place!" Viviana interrupts. Smiles. Gestures to snow, peaks.

Officers raise puzzled eyes. Nod. Stamp. Gesture. "Bienvenidos a Argentina!"

I ease out breath and clutch.

Viviana smiles. "See?

On a street in Bogota
by Syd Blackwell

Potato chips someone has dropped
now broken on a grimy walk
the ragged man bends low to ground
and sweeps the bits into a mound
his blackened fingers lift the crumbs
to bearded mouth with hunger numb
but passersby do not see this
his desperation they all miss

Bogotá, Colombia
03/07/12

The Marriage
by Helen Bing

New Zealand one week after our due sailing date. Generator problems. 3.45p.m., wearing our smartest clothes, my friends and I held on to our paper streamers - the norm for 1975.

A voice behind us said, "You'll be holding on to them for a long time."

"No," we replied. "We're sailing at 4."

"If you're right, I owe you drink, if not, you owe me one."

He was right - inside information.

A week to honour the bet.

Four weeks - getting serious!

Five months - a wedding on the other side of the world.

Forty-three years - still sailing.

Just off Sutter
by Alan Passey

Indigo sky morphed into dawn breaking cover onto Sutter. The chill smacked my cheeks. A steam vent hissed from the 'Frisco underworld. Lonely figures hunched to the early shift.

Somewhere I heard a radio. Classical music. Songs I couldn't tell. Heading away from the bay I found myself walking towards the radio, slowly getting louder.

Then there he was. Alone on an empty street, his voice chiming from the city walls sending deep rounded tones rolling out towards the morning. A tenor, singing for himself. For the joy of singing, and the solitary wanderer who just might happen by.

13 @ Thailand
by Sally Hewitt

On Koh Chang he shaves first signs of his adolescent moustache, breaks voice and masters a moped, all at breakneck speed.

Koh Samet persuades his bare feet, underwater dives, choosing calamari over cheeseburger.

In Bangkok he unglues his phone from his hand, eats chicken feet noodles with chopsticks.

Hua Hin hears him urging tuk-tuk drivers to "Lil! Lil!"and hurtling down Black Mountain waterslides.

In Pattaya he go-karts to winner, stacks it, laughs. His crowd handling and a wrong turn into Soi 6 raise one momentary blush.

Flying home, he rejects my nana hand. "Sal, I can handle turbulence now."

Ferry to Albania
by Vernon Lacey

A seabird hovered in the upper air, and then fell like an arrow, disappearing in the sea haze. I watched from a ferry deck as the boat chugged across the Ionian sea, Corfu distant, and the port of Saranda in Albania fast approaching. It was 1996. I'd volunteered for a summer-long, charity project renovating a maternity hospital in the north of the impoverished, ex-communist country. I'd read stories of violent gangs on remote roads. Ambushes. Dress like a pauper, we were told. In that hyphen of time, gliding over the sea, danger seemed impossible, and my heart was at peace.

To Be Young Again
by Sarah Owens

Siesta approaches and the busy streets of Granada empty. I find a quiet plaza and sit with a coffee and sugary churros. Water sprinklers gently saturate the air spreading a soft mist scented with jasmine.

"Senorita, I play for you?" I look up as a young man emerges from the shadows, his guitar slung low against his hip. He smiles at a beautiful girl sitting at the table opposite and, resting his foot on a chair, plays bold tremolo scales and flamenco rhythms. Vivid gypsy colours fill my mind, swirling skirts and stamping feet. Oh, to be young again.

A South American Conversation
by Mark Boyter

The dreadlocked young American in the Quito guesthouse leaned into her chair, cradling a *mate de coca*. "How many times you been robbed?"

I looked at her.

"Everyone I ask says they have," she said, "so I stopped asking 'If'." She took a sip.

"So, how many times?"

"Three," I said. "Bolivia twice, Ecuador once. My camera at the bus station in La Paz. My wallet in the market in Potosi. My watch on the bus to Guayaquil. Sitting in my seat, arm in the open window. Thief had to jump three feet."

She smiled and took another sip. "Everyone."

Amritha
by Brigid Gallagher

The temple guide placed two small medals featuring Sai Baba and Shirdi Sai, in the palms of my hand, before an amber liquid began to fill them from NOWHERE!

"Please drink," he urged.

I felt the taste of heavenly flowers tantalize my tongue, before my palms filled yet again with the delicious nectar.

"The liquid is known as Amritha," he continued.

I drank once more, as the wonder was repeated for a third and final time, then I handed him back the miracle producing medals.

"You enjoyed?

"It tasted divine," I replied.

I left the temple feeling incredibly blessed.

Drowning in Berlin
by Adrian Sturrock

I'm sitting in a bar with a friend, just a few hundred metres from a stretch of remaining Berlin Wall that flanks the river on this side of town. It's late October, it's well past dusk, and the rain that has consistently fallen since I arrived in this city is busy reflecting and animating the electric lights of surrounding buildings, passing cars, and the occasional glare of the overhead trains that intermittently rumble past our window. My first impression of this city is that it is hard, brutal, monochrome. Why then do I instantly feel comfortable here?

Diving the Mecca wreck
by Roger Knight

South Corniche Jeddah Saudi Arabia

In the muggy darkness, we gear up for the long reef walk out, where sting rays dart away from under our feet.

Finally, we drop down on to the Mecca, just as dawn breaks, spreading shafts of light that slowly dispels the darkness.

In her reclining position of final rest, in over 30 metres at her bow, she still holds her ill-fated cargo of rotting silk, that wave, like frayed coloured ribbons among the soft corals and fish that have now assumed permanent residence in this converted aquarium.

Let there be Dragons
by Deb Bott

Indonesia's 'Komodo Island' is not for the faint hearted. The tour briefing said: not to run if we had a dragon charging us 'yeah right'.

You smell them before you see them. Weighing in around 90 kilos and 3 meters long, the Komodo dragon is a frightening sight.

At the epi center eight dragons lazed in the hot sun. A staffer threw them some chicken carcasses and holy moly. All the dragons took off like grease lightening to get their share.

Now they were disturbed, crawling around the ground, slobbering, tongues smelling, they now wanted more and were looking at us!

Rock, Paper, Scissors
by Alan Packer

Spring sap urged a final swell to the Mallorcan olive root burrowing in a rock crack. Wood won and three tons of limestone crashed into the Torrent de Pareis.

We were not there, just scrambled over the evidence.

Then came water carrying a whole tree downward until it broke its trunk, smashing into boulders and stopping. Rock won. The torrent scoured it clean of bark.

We climbed over the trunk, afraid. The flood had gone but, trapped, we swam through the deep pools to escape. The cold scissored our breath.

It's a Small World
by Robyn Boswell

After a few weeks in the dryness of the Australian desert, Innot Hot Springs was an oasis, promising a chance to soak our weary bones. My sister and I soaked in the motel's hot outdoor pool under a cascade of stars, chatting to the only other guests, an Australian couple. Hearing we were from New Zealand, they said they only knew one person in New Zealand, in Dunedin, almost as far away from our home as it was possible to get. We only knew one person in Dunedin. Chatted further. Their friend was our friend's brother. Strange, but true!

All Roads Lead to Seligman
by James Robertson

"On this site in 1897," read the plaque, "nothing happened."

And nothing had happened since. Aside from the completion of Route 66.

Walking down the street I could smell the old burning rubber imbedded in the tarmac. It was as if every American car had passed through Seligman, and with it every American town too.

The hulks of re-painted vehicles lounged by the roadside. Number plates dotted the walls coloured with red, white and blue.

A pole stood directing me to Berlin, Melbourne, Glasgow and Rome. But road signs wouldn't let me forget; I was still on Route 66.

South American Rescue
by Delores Topliff

Our Jeepney reached the South American river town. After dust settled and people, pigs, and chickens departed, my 14-year-old son and I, here to help schools, looked for our contacts.

No-one.

There'd been some mistake.

A friend had written, "If anything goes wrong, find shopkeeper Antonio Anau."

My son guarded our luggage while I walked dusty streets asking for Antonio.

Clerks rattled off rapid-fire Spanish. He'd had surgery and was gone.

Dogs bite fearful people. I couldn't fear.

Finally, through another doorway, I glimpsed a man I'd seen once in the U.S.

In town for other reasons, he "rescued" us.

Vibrations
by Syd Blackwell

Winter driving in northern British Columbia is tough. My whole body was tingling. I found a motel. I just wanted to flop on the bed for an hour. I switched on the room light and then I saw it! I had a *Magic Fingers Vibrating Bed*! I´d never seen one. However, I didn't need more motion. I just flopped on the bed. And it started vibrating! Then it stopped. I got up, checked the bed, checked the coin box, and then warily lay back down. Nothing happened. Later, at the restaurant, everyone was talking about the small earthquake.

Croatia - land of lakes and waterfalls
by Gabi Reigh

Rastoke, the historic centre of Slunj in Croatia, is a fairy tale land of turquoise lakes and luminous cascades. As we started to explore it on our first morning, it offered a surprise at every turn. The river gurgled brightly over rocks, under dark-stained, medieval bridges, and as we followed its bend, we passed waterfall after waterfall, the place seeming more and more unreal, magical, beauty piling onto beauty, as if we'd opened a secret door and found ourselves cast as extras on the set of a Disney movie.

Water Melons
by Ronald Mackay

Both barren roads lead to Khebir. The coastal longer; the desert shorter.

I wait. The horizon yellow, shimmering.

Water melon-laden, a truck brakes.

"El Khebir?"

I climb up.

Pleased, he chooses desert. "Alone, I no risk!"

Blistering heat. An hour. A tire blows.

More nimble, I place the jack. I raise the axle on soft asphalt.

He sweats.

"Right!"

He wrestles.

Time slows. I watch as jack penetrates asphalt; as the differential approaches my skull.

He jams the wheel.

I breathe, crawl back into the sun.

Neither of us speak.

The sun smiles. The desert grins. "Got you now!"

Four, Please
by Nancy McBride

Moving in to my hotel in Saint Malo (FR), I'd barely crammed my suitcase, backpack and swaddled self into the antiquated, one-person elevator, and was selecting my floor when a shorter woman, swathed in a huge cape that swallowed her whole, stealthily insinuated herself in, too, her oozing cape filling any gaps. Compressed. Intimate. Awkward. Jerking, we haltingly ascended. Gears loudly cranking its load upwards, she looked up apologetically, "C'est petit."

I brightly replied, "Oui, mais automatic!"

Then we both smiled at our clever rhyme as we jolted to a stop, ultimately untangled and went our separate ways.

The Battambang Bamboo Train
by Alan Passey

When we dripped from the bus the track was clear.

Two paper thin men lifted a pair of loose axles onto the rails. A bamboo board loaded with a boat motor rested between them. An axle hooked to the motor with a cam belt.

Warily, we scrambled aboard, settling to the middle.

Thin Man One yanked the starter cord and we lurched, grabbing handholds.

"Must get to the station before the real train comes", shouted Thin Man Two above the din.

We hurtled along at ground level. I was ten years old again being fast, naughty and slightly dangerous.

In a Caravan Built for Two
by Helen Bing

Thirty-six hours from New Zealand to England, with 3 children, ready to spend our first night of our 3 month stay in my sister-in-law's 12 foot caravan. That included the tow bar!

We're jet lagged and overwhelmed after a day with the extended family.

We're tired.

Now it's just us, the luggage and the caravan. We need sleep.

The sling style top bunk for you my daughter.

The divan bed below is for you, my son.

In between Mum and Dad, young one.

Sleep well, one and all.

Frosty Morning, Scotland
by Robyn Boswell

The trees have sung the songs of autumn and now their bare, blackened fingers claw at the silver sky. Grass crunches under my feet and I brush swirls of white off the heather bushes lining the path. The long-horned red beasties by the fence breathe clouds into the frigid air and shake the snow out of their shaggy coats. I reach the tiny loch, ready to try my first ever step on a frozen pond. One step and a boom echoes through the still air as a crack opens up right across the loch. I jump back – not this time!

A Thai Swim
by Mark Boyter

My skin has turned the colour of hazelnuts. I float, and it glistens below the surface and catches the white filament lines from the sun. Nut brown in aqua. A wave laps into the sand, thins, dissolves, and is gone. Then another. Then quiet.

The steps at my hut are sandy and they burn against my bare feet. Coconut wood, baked silver and warped in the sun. It is just noon. Hang my towel on the clothesline. The horizon shimmers, azure over emerald. There is another island. The palms rustle, and then again, and then quiet. Like yesterday. Like tomorrow.

Welcome to Vietnam
by Sarah Owens

Waves of bicycles, trucks and rickshaws flow around me. I'm in Ho Chi Minh City the day before Tet and the crowds are vast. The scent of sweet incense and fried rice mingles with rotting fish and ammonia from the Saigon River. The streets blaze with sunflowers, lanterns glow and dancing dragons shimmy to a throbbing beat. At midnight golden fireworks illuminate the sky. A little girl dressed in Ao Dai embroidered with golden bamboo and peach blossom offers me candied ginger.

"Cam o'n ban," I try. She giggles and hides behind her mother.

Bahrain's Arab Spring
by Roger Knight

At the time, what created the most disquiet for me, at the height of the unrest, was not the unofficial road blocks manned by masked youths, the rubbish collecting in the streets, or even the Saudi militia flexing their muscle, but the visceral chanting at night.

Like an anthem of subjugation, it's potent protest would reverberate through me, to such an extent, that I had to wear earplugs, in order to get any sleep.

The energy conveyed, from the Shia villages around, felt so powerful, that no amount of tear gas, birdshot or military intervention could stop it.

Brief Encounter 2
by Dolores Banerd

In Bangkok, often I breakfast at an outdoor café that opens into a guesthouse. Mostly all I see are guests checking in and guests checking out, but today is different.

I was spooning my oatmeal when a bleary-eyed, silver-haired, sixtyish man —white —staggered out of his room bellowing, "She took my wallet, my watch, everything! Oh. My. God."

Not a muscle twitched on the Asian receptionist's stony face.

"I warned you many times not to bring Thai girls back to your room," she said.

Ah, a soap-dishy drama to enjoy along with my bland bowl of oatmeal. Lucky me!

Lochside
by James Robertson

I couldn't take my eyes off the view that the small reception of our hostel was blessed with.

The body of Loch Ness.

I made my way from the hostel down to the banks of the loch. The serene lake, made bright blue by the reflection of the clear sky, stretched out in front of me. Far on the other side was a lush forest, unimpeded by the man-made. From left to right, there was no end to the loch in sight.

It appeared to go on forever.

Underground
by Gouri Prakash

A baby lizard, slithering across the damp wall, froze in its tracks, as I shone my torch over it. The bat, however, decided to continue its meditation. 200 feet beneath the Earth's surface, I was inside the murky realms of Onandaga Caves.

Reddish-brown stalactites clung like unlit chandeliers, to the cave's ceiling. One hollow after another, a hut here, a hermit there, Nature's sculptures abounded and embellished. Constant drizzle suffused the musty air.

The door was the deformity. I pushed at it. Sunlight streamed. I stepped out. It felt, nothing short, of a rebirth, from the Earth's womb.

Come On
by Syd Blackwell

And are you interesting she began
as though the conversation had already
Are you interested he countered
Can you teach me something she persisted
I have been where you have not
Ah then you are a traveller
There are many ways to travel
And what ways have you travelled
I have travelled the ways of the eagle and the dove
the seeker and the lover
and walked the paths that only I may walk
Then let me walk the path to tomorrow
with you today
And interestingly he did

Cinderella in Përmet
by Elizabeth Gowing

My plate had been studded with amber, jade and ruby. These were Përmet's famous 'gliko' sweetmeats, made from walnut, aubergine and pumpkin.

The secret lies in first soaking the rinds in lime. Then they're boiled in sugar and lemon juice with geranium flowers to produce a tender, fragrant treat.

With lunch finished I was now trying another southern Albanian indulgence – the nearby warm springs.

There had been no-one at the natural pool, so I'd stripped and lolled here in the blue water feeling the sulphur-softness on my rejuvenated and sweetened skin; experiencing what can happen to pumpkins in Përmet.

The Blessing
by Alan Passey

We agreed that he was beautiful. The young shaven monk, twenty years old at most, amber robed and with skin as smooth as silk, sat smiling contentedly at the ungainly Westerners ranged before him. Each of us would receive a blessing, when, in turn, we shuffled forward, place our palms together and bend in supplication. He acknowledged each ungainly wobble on knees no longer fit for purpose.

A short prayer in Khmer, for our knees, probably. A red band tied around our wrists to signify the blessing.

Six weeks later I still wear the band. My knees are holding out.

Broome, Western Australia
by Helen Bing

Early this morning, the sun had turned the water a gentle turquoise, and the silvery light danced on the surface. Now the tide has filled the bay and the colour has intensified. A light breeze touches the surface.

The coastline that this morning sizzled with rich reds have now morphed into softer, sandy tones by the sun's shadows. Scraggy trees silhouette the clear skyline. Gulls screech across the water.

It's raw. It's pristine. It's Western Australia.

A Number Followed by Lots of Zeros
by Ronald Mackay

"For your expenses, Sir. Please sign."

The wad of twenty-eight million pastel-coloured Rupiah notes surprised me by their modesty.

I signed; locked most in my room-safe; attended my appointment.

"We'll talk in the gardens created when Java was Dutch."

We planned, reviewed, agreed all project details.

A screech, irate, blocked my exit from the restroom. The official hand demanded payment due. Uncertain, I selected a pretty note. A number followed by lots of zeros. The screech transformed into a prayer, hands pressed together in recognition of the divinity in me.

For whoever tips a year's earnings indeed must be divine.

See you later, Alligator
by Katie Parry

Disney World Florida. A whirl of candyfloss and creepy mouse costumes. In the Everglades, we can finally breath. Canoeing with alligators is to be the highlight. Alas, I get over-competitive during a race home and tip myself and my mother into the swamp. Panic! We thrash around, desperate to get out of the water. Our passports sink without trace. Back on dry land, I am in disgrace. My penance? To sit for hours turning individual pages of our weed-covered bird book to stop them from sticking together. And, much worse, no sour jelly beans for the rest of the holiday.

Berlin East
by Adrian Sturrock

The bar is ambiguously lit, allowing each table complete anonymity amongst the dark corners of the room. I laughingly describe the décor as 'heroin-chic'; it is stark and decaying. This isn't my usual type of haunt, but I do find comfort in it. The graffiti that has grown like wild ivy outside, consuming concrete and metal, appears to have spread its way in through the doorway and infected every aspect of the building with its imperative to communicate. It's ugly; it's unflinching; it's reassuring. It says that Berlin is owned by its people, not by statesmen or sterile corporations.

Malady in Moresby Papua New Guinea
by Roger Knight

Nothing is more nightmarish, that to succumb to some debilitating tropical illness far from home. For me, this experience was made worse, as, back in the early 70's, the only hospital in Port Moresby, was a leprosorium.

Waiting to be seen by the doctor, among the lepers, with their melted faces and withered limbs, along with Papuan women, suckling piglets with their bare breasts, made me think that this was a fate worse than death.

In my hand, I desperately clutched my appointment card, which to my further horror, was in fact intended for use as a morgue tag.

Elephants
by Sarah Owens

Scrambling up a termite mound I watch a mother elephant wade into the Zambezi river, but her family hesitate. She sucks in water and swirls her trunk spraying them. The herd join her, but a bull calf remains on the bank. His mother winds her trunk around his body and coaxes him in to join the fun, all the time she strokes and encourages him. As they move away, the mother flaps her ears and turns her gentle eyes towards me. She's not threatening, just acknowledging my presence. They move off silently into the dense Zimbabwean bushveld and disappear.

Bear out of Nowhere
by James Robertson

"If we saw a bear," said Sally, "I'd just run."

Anything was possible. The dense forests could conceal any predator Yosemite might throw at us.

As we drove, cars in front began slowing down until we had stopped.

"What's wrong?"

Sightseers leapt from vehicles, clutching their cameras. We tentatively followed, past the parked cars to the travellers by the roadside. And there she was. A body of rippling brown fur lumbered in the green meadow. Her ears twitched as she sniffed through the shrubbery.

Awestruck; we couldn't even bring ourselves to take a photo. All we could do was stare.

St Mark's Square, Venice 1975
by Robyn Boswell

In awe to actually be in the magnificence of St Mark's Square, we gather together in a huddle around our guide, Bill. None of us notices the elderly gentleman hovering on the edges of our group. Bill continues extolling the virtues and history of this fascinating, ancient city. Finally, he announces "Venice is sinking at the rate of a few centimetres a year."

The elderly gent pushes through the crowd, clenches his fist, waves it in Bill's face. His voice rises in anger. "Veneeze is not a-sinking! Veneeze is not a-sinking!"

His words still echo down through the years.

There's nothing funny about the philtrum
by Mark Boyter

When you are in Pokhara, Nepal, in a two-chair wood frame barber shop getting a straight razor shave, and after the barber has lathered your whiskers and dabbed your moustache and stropped the razor and proved it once, twice, through a square of paper and scraped clean your throat and cheeks and he takes you by the nostrils and pulls your head back and presses the blade firm against the hollow of tightened skin above your lip and in the mirror you see your friend pull his nose and snort, the most important thing to remember is not to laugh.

Tokyo Twilight
by Suzy Pope

Steam from the yakitori grill blurred the mushroom parade of umbrellas down Omoide Yokocho. Rain lashed Tokyo's streets.

Quietly sipping an Asahi, I planned my escape. Salarymen with rumbled shirts and loose ties passed around a microphone.

"Billy Jean is not my brother," they screeched to tinny beats.

I'd accidentally crashed an anniversary party.

The microphone reached my end of the bar. I stood up to leave, but red-faces pleaded with me. I was 5,000 miles from home. Nobody knew me. I sang my heart out, off-key. They bought me enough Saki to see me through to 5am.

Sunset
by Syd Blackwell

From the sandstone bluffs
that rise abruptly
above the sand at Atlántida
the summer sun had not yet set
From the perspective of the beach
it was just disappearing
and a ripple of clapping
rolled into a wave
A mostly standing ovation
for this day's duration
thank you for the sun now done
Applause crept up the bluffs
until all about me
homage was paid
to the sun
for the day it had made

Just 24 hours - Paris to Amiens
by Elizabeth Moore

An early train from Gare du Nord. The hotel waitress named Matilda. World cup games streaming in the foyer. An early start to Hamel. Site of the 93-minute battle. An allied victory. The trenches still outlined in the soil. Surrounded by wheatfields. Poppies growing among the sugar beet. Driving to Villers-Bretonneux. Passing the lonely road taken to battle. The graves in white military rows. The beloved family name chiseled in marble. A time to talk to one never met. Tears for the life never lived in full. Lest We Forget.

CONTRIBUTORS

Adrian Sturrock

Adrian Sturrock is a writer, occasional musician, teacher, and ethnic minority (except when in Wales), specialising mostly in observation and unconsidered opinion. He currently lives in Buckinghamshire, England, with wife, Natalie: his travel companion best friend, and the person responsible for keeping him out of trouble on social media. Adrian has written articles for a variety of online publications, as well as having excerpts of his poetry/lyrics displayed alongside those of Benjamin Zephaniah in Luton Town Hall. His first book, *The Sat Nav Diaries* has achieved a string of 5-star reviews on both sides of the Atlantic, resulting in it being nominated for the 2018 Kindle book Awards. His second book, *RANDOM*, is due for release in February 2019.

Alan Packer

Alan Packer developed travel writing based on vivid experiences of living and working in Kosovo. In 2010 he started a family blog called *Runjeva* describing every day incidents and events. From this, friends encouraged him to explore writing more seriously and to seek a wider audience. In 2017 he won the Bradt New Travel Writer of the Year Award with a short story: *The Village Sledge Run*. Alan and his wife Mary now live in the Scottish Borders.

Alan Passey

If there's one place Alan Passey and his wife have fallen in love with it is India. But there's so much world to explore. Alan has become known for his cycling adventures, specifically cycling across Spain, and has received good reviews for his first travel book "Crossing Spain - wandering in the land of the bull".

Alison Galilian

I was born and brought up in Scotland but left in my early twenties. I've worked and travelled in Greece, Turkey, Spain, Poland, Israel, Egypt, most of Asia, Australia and Africa. I love travel - the more adventurous the better, but since the birth of my daughter, I have had to settle down and become an armchair traveller instead! I currently live in rural England with my husband, daughter and two rescue cats.

Alyson Hilbourne

Alyson has spent the last thirty years living and working overseas. She writes short stories and travel pieces and has been published in magazines in the UK and online. She loves travelling and sells short stories to fund her addiction.

Amy L. Bovaird

Amy Bovaird comes from northwestern Pennsylvania, which she's dubbed 'the land of eternal winter.' She taught English as a Second Language (ESL) abroad and in the United States for many years. Amy lives with a dual disability—progressive vision and hearing loss due to Usher Syndrome, a rare inherited condition that leads to deaf blindness.

Amy is an accomplished public speaker on a variety of topics based on her life experiences and continues to educate and inspire others through her writing and speaking.

She has authored three memoirs: *Mobility Matters: Stepping Out in Faith, Cane Confessions: The Lighter Side to Mobility, and Seeking Solace.*

Amy also blogs and manages to find humor around almost every corner. You can learn more about her at www.amybovaird.com.

Andrew Klein

Andy Klein was born in New York and raised in southern California. He graduated from San Diego State University, and, after attaining his master's degree in psychology, spent the next fifteen years traveling around the world. He taught children in Japan and Taiwan as well as here, in the states. Inspired by his youngest son, he has begun to write a series of children's books. He now lives with his family north of Atlanta.

Angie Clifford

Angie was born south of the river Thames on the 6th March 1951; therefore she considers herself a Londoner, (her great grandfather acted alongside Charlie Chaplin on the London music hall theatres in the early 1900's).

Her mother; abandoned as a three-week-old baby, and subsequently raised by her grandmother and a spinster aunt, was a naive twenty-three-year-old when she married. Having no idea where babies came from, Angie's birth was a momentous occasion, so much so she thought her new child was an Angel, so she called her Angela, which translates as Gods messenger and was also a popular name in the 1950's.

As every generation does Angie rejected the lifestyle of her parents and made a vow to be different...maybe perfect, the arrogance of youth! She married at nineteen to Jerry, four years older than herself, she saw him as mature, her knight in shining armour...And the rest as they say is history.

Angie and Jerry have four children and five grandchildren; so far! They are now retired and live between UK, and Spain, enjoying the indulgent life.

Anu Devi

Dr. Anu Devi was born in Fiji. She grew up in California, USA where she completed her undergraduate in the medical sciences. After working for a few years at a law firm in the environment and natural resources area, she went to the University of Oxford in the UK to complete her Masters in Environmental Change and Management, and her Doctorate in Public Health and Social Policy. She has worked in the public-private sector including in the field of Smart Cities, International Development, Operational Intelligence, Internet of Things and Risk Management. She is interested in a wide range of topics because she believes people live in an interconnected world and nothing operates in silos. She also has a passion for travel, photography, yoga and meditation.

Apple Gidley

A transient life has seen Apple Gidley live in countries as diverse as Papua New Guinea and Thailand, or Equatorial Guinea and Trinidad & Tobago, and another eight in between. Her memoir, *Expat Life Slice by Slice* (Summertime Publishing 2012), chronicles the highs and lows of that nomadic life - one she wouldn't trade for all the proverbial tea in one of the places she hasn't lived, China.

Her travel articles are filled with colour and spiced with cultural subtleties which take the arm-chair-traveller to that country, or make the experienced traveller add it to their list, and she has short stories published in various anthologies.

Her blog can be found at www.applegidley.wordpress.com.

Gidley's first novel, *Fireburn*, set in the 1870s Danish West Indies (now the US Virgin Islands) was published (OC Publishing, Canada) in October 2017 and continues to receive 5* reviews. The sequel, *Transfer*, which takes the characters through to the American purchase of the Danish West Indies in 1917, will be released in March 2019.

She currently divides her time between St Croix in the US Virgin Islands and Houston, Texas.

Barbara Hunt

Barbara says, 'I enjoy travelling, particularly to countries where the culture is vastly different to my own. I have had a few successes with flash fiction, short stories, memoir, and essay, but this is the first time I've written a travel piece.

Ben Stamp

Ben Stamp was born in Tokyo, Japan, and raised in North Little Rock, Arkansas. Insects with stingers cause him to make childish noises. When he is not travelling, he lives in Catalonia.

Bonnie Jean Warren

Bonnie Jean is a poet and creative writer residing in Brooklyn, NY. She has just finished compiling her memoir of near-death experiences soon to be published. Bonnie has traveled to over 35 countries, has a Bachelor of Journalism and a Diploma in Acting for Film. Currently, she works an English teacher in Manhattan.

Brigid Gallagher

Brigid P. Gallagher aspired to becoming a doctor, but God had other plans!

In 1986, she embarked on a series of studies to become one of the first natural medicine practitioners in Scotland. She eventually became a tutor for a number of community projects, a women's prison, and the Open Studies and Summer Schools of Stirling University from 1993 to 1999.

In 1999, she relocated to Donegal, Ireland – the home of her ancestors. Four years later she succumbed to a mystery illness which was eventually diagnosed as fibromyalgia.

Stopping the World forced Brigid to reassess her life, and creative writing became a significant part of her healing process.

She retrained in organic horticulture and taught this subject in schools until 2016.

"Watching the Daisies – Life Lessons on the Importance of Slow" was written to inspire others on their self-healing journey.

Brigid blogs at https://watchingthedaisies.com.

Cat Jenkins

Cat Jenkins lives in the Pacific Northwest where the weather is often conducive to long hours before a keyboard. Her stories in humor, fantasy, speculative fiction and horror have been published both online and in print. Her first novel, "Sara When She Chooses," was published May 2018.

On Twitter: @CatJenkins11

Celia Dillow

Celia spent 5 years in South America; it changed everything. Now settled in SW Britain, she reads and writes travel stories, is the author of an award-winning local wildlife blog and is proud that her story about taking a shaggy dog to Argentina is included in Bradt's most recent anthology. She is a specialist dyslexia teacher during term time and a traveller, writer, birdwatcher and hiker during the school holidays.

Colleen MacMahon

I live in the West Country of England, surrounded by a wealth of rural beauty which inspires a lot of my work as a watercolour artist. I'm also an actress, audiobook narrator and writer. Travel, natural history and culture have always been my passions, preferably in the company of family, friends and a large tub of quality ice cream!

Deb Bott

If someone said to me 30 years ago, I would be a sailor exploring the world's oceans in my 50's, I would have laughed in their face!

Until the year 2000 my entire boating experience was an overnight trip on a ferry from Melbourne to Tasmania at the tender age of 12. During 2000 to 2009 my partner and I pottered about Moreton Bay, Queensland in three different sailing boats. In 2010 we sold our home, bought and moved aboard our beloved *Matilda*.

We retired in 2014 to enjoy sailing the east coast of Australia. We have since sailed south to Eden, New South Wales and to the most northern point of Australia to Cape York.

2016 was the year we left Australia bound for South East Asia, exploring Indonesia, Malaysia, Singapore, Thailand and Borneo/Indonesia. My sailing experiences are what I base my writing on.

Our journey can be followed at: www.svmatilda.com.

Delores Topliff

Delores Topliff is a college teacher and writer who loves to travel and keeps her passport dusted off and ready for use. She is a native-born American who married a Canadian so also enjoys being a Canadian citizen. She divides her year between living in Minnesota with family and NE Mississippi where it's warmer and family likes to come visit. Contact her at delorestopliff.com or on Facebook.

Dolores Banerd

I'm Dolores, and I was born in Canada on a large wheat farm in southern Saskatchewan. When I was four, my parents relocated to Vancouver, British Columbia, and I decided to go with them. After attending college there and brief sojourns in London, England, Toronto and Winnipeg, I was moved to move to a city that tops them all in sunshine, Los Angeles. At the moment, my passport is dusty, but I have traveled extensively —often on my own—in Europe and more recently throughout Southeast Asia, Indonesia, and India.

Elizabeth Gowing

Elizabeth Gowing has lived in Albania for the last five years. She is the co-founder of The Ideas Partnership charity working in the Balkans on education, environmental and cultural heritage projects, and the author of four books on the region. Her translations from Albanian to English have been published by Rrokullia Press. She is a frequent contributor to BBC Radio 4's 'From Our Own Correspondent'.

Elizabeth Moore

Elizabeth has lived in Australia all her life. She is happily married, a mother of two, grandmother of five and devoted assistant to one very bossy tortoiseshell cat named Lucy. Her working career began as a speech pathologist and later morphed into the totally unrelated field of retail manager in a university science centre and planetarium.

Travel has always been a focus and yes – there has always been a bucket list. This was brought into stark relief when she was diagnosed with breast cancer and following treatment, a travel timetable began to take shape. Guam was first, followed quickly by European and North American adventures. Illness nudged another long-held interest to the fore and Elizabeth began chronicling her trips with extensive photography, promising herself she would also write about her exploits.

Frank Kusy

Born and raised in the fog-shrouded streets of 1960s London, and with more than 30 years of travel writing experience under his belt, aspiring Buddhist and incorrigible cat-lover Frank Kusy is constantly leaping out of his bed at night to write down book ideas before he forgets them. Some of them lead to good things, like his humorous series of travel memoirs set in India/SouthEast Asia and his quirky 'Ginger the Gangster Cat' book, which won a Gold Medal in 2015 for middle graders. Many others lead to nightmares, however, since he often can't read his own handwriting in the mornings. Nevertheless, his books have received international press acclaim and have made the Kindle Top 100 List several times. He likes to write to make people smile.

Check out Frank's book store at: frankkusybooks.weebly.com.

Gabi Reigh

Gabi Reigh is an English teacher at a sixth form college in Hampshire. She uses her well-earned holidays to travel, read and translate novels and poetry.

Gouri Prakash

Gouri seizes every opportunity there is, to travel in order to discover and re-discover the world that we live in and to write about it.

Hannah Standen

Hannah Standen is an Australian writer currently based in London, England. As an adventure seeker and explorer at heart, she spends any chance she can travelling the world.

Helen Bing

Kia ora. My name is Helen Bing. I live in Auckland, New Zealand, and like many of my contemporaries, I am rediscovering the wonders of travelling. These days we do a lot of our travelling by sea which gets us to all sorts of interesting parts of the world.

James Robertson

My name is James Robertson and I am a young writer and traveller. I have decided to combine two of my great passions into one by channelling some of my recent gap year adventures into travel writing excerpts. I am traditionally a playwright and run the amateur theatre company "Plain English Theatre Company" in Melbourne, Australia.

Katie Parry

Katie Parry is an aspiring writer who longs to give up her day job and retire to a cottage by the sea with her two (currently imaginary) dogs and her (also often imaginary) notebooks. Katie was brought up in the Scottish Highlands and loves mountains and swimming in cold water. She has lived in the UK, France, Sierra Leone, Kenya, South Africa and the USA.

Lee P. Ruddin

Lee is a Birkenhead born, Birmingham-based perennial student who currently works in the security industry in the UK.

He wrote his first travel piece five years ago on crossing the Atlantic (westwards) aboard Queen Mary II and now, aged 35, aspires to be master of one trade rather than a jack of all by entering the travel sector.

Lindsay de Feliz

Lindsay de Feliz was born, raised and educated in the UK, where she worked in London as a marketing lecturer and a Marketing Director for various financial service companies. In her mid-40s, she decided to follow her dreams and travel the world as a scuba diving instructor, ending up in the Dominican Republic 17 years ago.

She was on a six-month contract but fell in love with the country and its people and met and married a Dominican. Having been shot in the throat during a robbery she was unable to dive any more, and now works as a writer, translator and marketing consultant.

Lindsay currently lives in the northeast mountains in the Dominican Republic with her husband, four dogs, one cat, six goats, two geese and numerous chickens. She writes a blog about the Dominican Republic and daily life at www.yoursaucepans.blogspot.com and is the author of the bestselling books "What about your saucepans?" and "Life After My Saucepans".

Lu Barnham

Lu Barnham is the author of two books: 'An African Alphabet' chronicles her journey across Africa by public transport while 'The Cicada's Summer Song' describes her 1200km solo walking pilgrimage to Shikoku's 88 temples, Japan. Born in Yorkshire, Lu now lives in New South Wales, Australia. To follow her travels, visit www.lubarnham.com.

Madeline Sharples

Madeline Sharples is the author of, *Leaving the Hall Light On: A Mother's Memoir of Living with Her Son's Bipolar Disorder and Surviving His Suicide*, in prose and poetry (Dream of Things). She also co-authored *Blue-Collar Women: Trailblazing Women Take on Men-Only Jobs* (New Horizon Press), co-edited the poetry anthology, *The Great American Poetry Show*, Volumes 1, 2, and 3, and wrote the poems for two photography books, *The Emerging Goddess* and *Intimacy* (Paul Blieden, photographer). Her poems have appeared online and in print magazines and journals. Madeline's articles have appeared on the Huffington Post, Naturally Savvy, PsychAlive, Aging Bodies, and Open to Hope websites. She also posts at her blog, Choices (madelinesharples.com). She is currently working on a novel.

Malcolm D. Welshman

Malcolm Welshman is a retired vet and author. He was the My Weekly vet for 15 years and has written many features for magazines such as She, The Lady, The People's Friend, Cat World, Yours, and newspapers such as The Sunday Times and the Daily Mail. He is the author of three pet novels, the first of which, Pets in a Pickle, reached number two on Kindle's bestseller list. His third novel, Pets Aplenty, was a finalist for The People's Book Prize 2015. A memoir, An Armful of Animals, was published in September 2018; and through a collection of twenty stories tells how animals have shaped his life as a vet. Malcolm is also an international speaker on cruise ships, a regular BBC Radio Somerset panellist, and a bi-monthly contributor to a local community radio, Keep 106 in Dorset.

Website: http://www.malcolmwelshman.co.uk.

Mark Boyter

Mark is a traveller and writer and a marathon runner. He loves wine with a good mouth-feel, films that make him laugh, and a good rack of BBQ ribs (which begs the question; is there such a thing as a bad rack of BBQ ribs?). His first book, the travel memoir *Crescent Moon Over Laos,* was published in 2014. His other writing includes smaller travel pieces and of the commonalities and influences that shape and inform our individual and collective lives. A college instructor by training, Mark has lived and taught in both Nagoya and Kyoto, Japan, the Emirate of Sharjah in the UAE, and both Toronto and Vancouver in Canada. At 59, he finally took the plunge and married his long-term partner. He lives, with increasing contentedness, in Richmond, British Columbia, with his new wife and their two cats, and when he isn't running or writing or drinking wine, tends the grape vines in their garden and marvels at what sun and water and time can create.

Mary Mae Lewis

Mary Mae is author of the novel *Where There's a Will, There's a Woman*. She has kept a diary since she was sixteen and is a prolific letter writer.

Raised in Staffordshire UK, she trained to be a primary school (PE and English) teacher and later qualified as TEFLA teacher.

She lived in Wales for one year, London two years, Grand Cayman four years (where she worked as a newspaper reporter) and Malawi for five years.

She now lives in Newcastle-u-Lyme UK but spends half the year in Southern Spain.

Married for nearly 50 years she has three sons and four grandchildren.

It is from personal experience that her fiction is born.

She has been published In THE TELEGRAPH, is a published poet and has won prizes in short story competitions.

Website: www.author-marymaelewis.co.uk.

Mike Cavanagh

Mike Cavanagh is now in his sixties and has no idea how he got here. He lives with his wife, Julie, and two black cats in Bateman's Bay, NSW. The house he and Julie live in is quirky and in need of regular maintenance, as are its owners. Mike's passions are writing, playing guitar, composing music, and, as Julie will only too readily tell you, playing too many role-playing games on PC. Find out more about Mike's memoirs *One of its Legs are Both the Same* and *A Pocket Full of Days* on his site: http://oneofitslegs.org.

Nancy McBride

Perception. Perspective. Twists. Humor. These, to me, are essences to storytelling. As Tim O'Brien revealed to me in The Things They Carried, stories are not what happened, they are what happened *to you*!

Things happen to me. Examples? A man fell from the ceiling onto my head in a restaurant. A kangaroo in a pink shirt bounced across the road in front of me in the outback of Australia. I scored a bull's eye rifle-shooting in The Urals. I was struck by lightning. The Queen Mum was tattooed on my bum. I learned how to "be seen", was "pregnant" with pop-corn, and put a sign on my car, "MASSACHUSETTS OR BUST". Those sub-titles are just scraping the surface of the kind of ordinary-for-me experiences I inhabit. Doors suddenly open and I trip into the next dimension, illustrating to me that there are obviously an infinite number of dimensions. They don't scare me. I've had a near death experience. I'm a walking happening. Perception. Perspective.

Being present to interpret my life and to allow it to "happen" is my shtick. I've travelled. I've fallen. I'm a disaster. I'm a survivor. I've ruminated. I've worked. I've loved. I've raised kids. I blurt art. Life's a story happening.

Check out Nancy's fascinating art on her web page: QUIRKY R US ARTWORK.

Patricia Steele

I'm a west coast girl that moved to the east coast and back again. Twice. My imagination has always been etched in music, color and rose-colored glasses. I've had crazy characters and stories banging and fluttering around in my head, dying to get out, since I was old enough to hold a pen. I'm a fan of historical fiction filled with adventure and romance. And I'm addicted to genealogy! My sense of humor runs a little rampant at times, I'm no stranger to laughter, and I love a good anticipation scene. I am proud to state that *The Girl Immigrant*, the first novel in my Spanish Pearls Series, is now translated into Spanish and Italian.

She is an administrator for the Hawaiian Spaniards Facebook site, a member of the Arizona Genealogical Society and a volunteer for the Find-A-Grave organization. Taking a break from genealogy research, she returned to her first love in writing: FICTION, with a touch of romance between the pages.

In between writing, research and flower pots, she enjoys wine, traveling and her family. To read more about Patricia, please check her author's page at:

www.patriciabbsteele.com.

Philip East

I am Phil. I sometimes write, though not as much as I would like to; I have a blog called bewilderedbee.com, though it never seems to match my expectations; I travel a lot, but procrastinate more, and I am so awkward that I simply cannot write about myself in the third person.

Rob Johnson

Rob Johnson is an author and reluctant olive farmer who lives in Greece on a remote five-acre smallholding with his wife Penny, six rescue dogs, two cats and four hundred and twenty olive trees.

Having been a professional playwright many years ago, he has since turned his hand to writing books. The most recent is 'A Kilo of String', which is all about his and Penny's often bizarre experiences of living in Greece for the past fourteen years. Variously reviewed as "Fabulously funny - a real must for lovers of all things Greek" and "The best of the 'moved abroad' books I can remember reading", 'A Kilo of String' is loosely based on his podcast series of the same name, episodes of which are free to listen to on his website at https://rob-johnson.org.uk.

Rob's previous three books are all novels. 'Lifting the Lid' and 'Heads You Lose' are comedy thrillers, the latter being mainly set in Greece, and 'Quest for the Holey Snail' is a comedy time travel adventure, which is mainly set in Ancient Greece.

Robyn Boswell

I live in the beautiful far north of New Zealand surrounded by beaches and forests. My family have lived here since the earliest days of settlement in New Zealand.

I love travelling and have been lucky to have explored many fascinating parts of our wonderful world. I've visited America many times and stayed with wonderful friends I have made. I lived and worked in Scotland, the land of my ancestors, mostly clearing tables and washing dishes in a slightly questionable restaurant, a million miles from my job as a teacher in New Zealand. My greatest adventure was 3 months camping and 20,000kms around the Outback and Tropics of Australia. Nowadays it's all about rediscovering my own beautiful country and discovering the joys of cruising. Travel has truly broadened my mind.

Roger Knight

I have lived and worked in around 15 countries and having recently retired, I have finally got around to writing about some of my experiences spent in several exotic and far flung destinations. I have spent a third of my life in Australasia, so consequently have quite a bit of varied experience to draw from, as regards that region of the world.

Ronald Mackay

As a very young man and later, throughout his professional life, Ronald Mackay travelled widely, living and working for lengthy periods within social and political cultures quite different to those of his native Scotland. He turned back to a more creative form of writing after having taught in universities for three decades and undertaken many evaluations of international programmes that promoted community development, education and agricultural research and development. He has written and published two memoirs, one remembering with affection his work in banana plantations on the island of Tenerife in 1960/61, the other recounting his experiences behind the Iron Curtain in Ceaușescu's Romania at the height of the Cold War. He has also enjoyed productions and readings of his plays for community theatre. After farming in Argentina from 2003 to 2012, Ronald and his Peruvian wife now live in a house they built together on Rice Lake near the small community of Keene in Ontario, Canada.

Sally Hewitt

Sally Hewitt, Norfolk, UK

Mum-nag to four, besotted nana-slave to four more. A published non-fiction writer. I love travelling, anywhere, enjoy writing, professionally. Redundancy this year provides freedom and opportunity to combine both, leisurely.

Two days after this holiday 13 (in the photo with me) messaged me to say thank you for it. It was a sweet message, written in 13 language, 'Sal. Yer Netflix has run out'.

Sarah Owens

Sarah discovered her love of solo travel in her fifties and since then has cycled across Vietnam, seen the sunrise over the Himalayas and the sun set behind the Taj Mahal. Her travels have taken her from Africa to Australia, New Zealand, The South Pacific and Thailand to name but few. And, she's not done yet.

Sourabha Rao

Sourabha Rao is a writer from Mysuru, currently living in Bengaluru. A Computer Science Engineer who worked in the IT industry after graduation, she quit her job to pursue her passion. She is now the Staff Writer at India's leading travel-and-photography company, Toehold. She is an avid reader, a capricious poet and an Earth-lover who travels to not only popular destinations but is also in constant search for offbeat places that don't make it to popular maps, so that she could write about them for those who possess the common fierce love for this Pale Blur Dot, our only home.

Sunny Lockwood

Sunny Lockwood lives with her husband in the Blue Ridge Mountains of Western North Carolina (U.S.A.). Both retired, they write travel memoirs about their various adventures. Their books, available at Amazon.com, have won awards and fans from around the world.

Some of Sunny's favorite authors: Laura Ingalls Wilder, Loren Eiseley, Viktor Frankl, John Steinbeck and Alexander McCall Smith.

Her heroes include Albert Schweitzer, Nelson Mandela, Vaclav Havel, Prudence Crandall and Harriet Tubman.

Susan Mellsopp

Susan Mellsopp is retired and lives with her golden retriever guide dog Jay in Hamilton New Zealand. She recently joined a writer's group and is being challenged to write in genres other than travel and memoir. She has published two school histories and writes for the New Zealand Blind Foundation as well as an Australian travel website. She is a voracious reader, loves to travel, listen to classical music, cook, and enjoys learning to use modern technology.

Suzy Pope

Suzy Pope likes the boring parts of travel best. Timetables, waiting rooms, long train journeys, planning, and research. It's probably because she's a librarian as well as a freelance travel writer. She's taken some of the longest, rockiest, most scenic and luxurious trains in the world and delighted in planning every second of the journey.

Syd Blackwell

I was born in a little ski town that used to be a gold mining town in the mountains of southeastern British Columbia. I also lived on the coast, on Vancouver Island, in the north, and even in northern Alberta for a decade. I visited every province and territory in Canada, and more than 40 other countries. I was an educator, an innkeeper, and an assisted living facilitator. My life was rich with experiences before I left Canada less than two months before my 61st birthday.

Uruguay has been our home for more than a decade. My wife and I share our home with our five dogs. And quite a few visitors. We have found time in our retirement to do things we never seemed to find time to do before. I have found time to be a writer and an artist. Both give me great pleasure. We have continued to travel, particularly in South America.

Tom Czaban

Tom is a British ex-pat living in the Czech Republic. He particularly enjoys writing about travel and cross-cultural differences. You can find more of his writing at www.tomczaban.com.

Valerie Fletcher Adolph

Valerie Fletcher Adolph was born and raised in England, but has lived in British Columbia, Canada for many years. She tries hard not to believe that she is old enough to know better.

Vernon Lacey

At the Beatles Museum, Liverpool, standing next to George Harrison's guitar

I grew up in Cheshire, UK. I teach Philosophy, Drama, and English in Munich. Before moving to Germany, I taught in Barcelona where I met my German wife. We have three children, Hannah, Myriam, and Aódhán.

Vernon is the author of 'South to Barcelona' published by Ant Press (September 2018).

Wenlin Tan

Wenlin Tan is an interdisciplinary artist, illustrator and writer from Singapore. Her short story 'The giant & the bird' & accompanying illustrations have been published by Epigram books Singapore in an anthology. Her illustrated short story 'The droplet' was showcased at Singapore Art book fair & the original painting will be exhibited at House of Vans, London as part of Blue dot Generation.

You can find more of her work on her website www.wenlintan.com and her instagram @wenlintellsstories.

For the story she has shared, Wenlin was in Ishinomaki as part of a program, in partnership with Sosei Partners - http://soseipartners.com.

Thank you!

I trust you have enjoyed this brand-new collection of travel stories and highlights.

If you did, then please leave a review on Amazon, even if it is only a few words. Thank you!

Please check out the fd81.net blog for competition updates throughout the year. You can also e-mail me at fd81@assl.co.uk with any questions or to get advance notice of upcoming contests and new releases.

Many thanks to the authors, writers and poets that have contributed and given their whole-hearted support to this publication.

Previous Editions of Travel Stories and Highlights

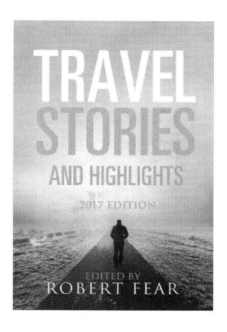

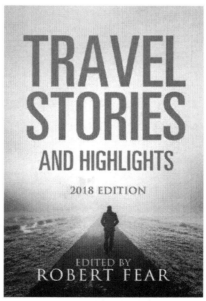

Both books are available on Amazon in Kindle and Paperback formats.

About the Editor

Robert Fear has lived in Eastbourne, on the south coast of the UK for half his life. He moved there to be with Lynn, his future wife and is still there with her thirty years later. As cat-lovers they have taken on several rescue cats over the years and are currently owned by three - Hazell (tabby), Jet (black) and Sparky, a bouncy ginger two-year-old.

For his day job Robert works as a self-employed software consultant. In his spare time, he writes, edits and self-publishes books, and organises annual travel writing competitions.

Robert's interest in travel goes back to his twenties when he spent most of his time abroad. His experiences included; a summer in Ibiza, hitch-hiking around Europe and touring the USA & Canada. His most eventful trip was in 1981 when he travelled around Asia.

Born into a religious sect known as the Exclusive Brethren, his father John took the brave step of leaving it with his young family when Robert was nine years old. Robert never saw his grandparents again but is thankful for being able to grow up outside this restrictive group. His life has been full of adventures that he would never have experienced otherwise.

Books by Robert Fear

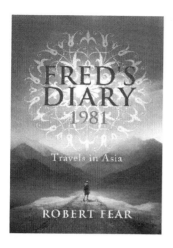

Fascinating time capsule from the 80's

Have you ever wanted to read someone else's diary?

Would you like to experience travelling in Asia without leaving home?

Then this book is for you. Fred's Diary 1981 is a fascinating insight into a young man's travels around Asia in the early 1980's. This is a unique opportunity to delve into Fred's daily diary, which details the 158 days he spent travelling around Asia. Follow Fred throughout his extensive travels to Hong Kong, Thailand, India and Nepal.

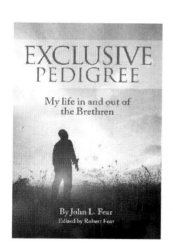

John Fear was born into a religious sect known as the Exclusive Brethren. This sheltered him from the outside world as he grew up, but could not hide him from its influences. A struggle began in his mind that led him to leave the Brethren, along with his young family. This is a story that was always meant to be told. During his later life John Fear had prepared a lot of the book, along with notes for chapters that he knew would not be completed. It is only now, over twenty years later, that the book has finally been published.

Both books are available on Amazon in Kindle and Paperback formats.

Made in the USA
San Bernardino, CA
23 April 2019